BRITISH STEAM
MILITARY CONNECTIONS:
LNER STEAM LOCOMOTIVES
& TORNADO

BRITISH STEAM MILITARY CONNECTIONS:

LNER STEAM LOCOMOTIVES & TORNADO

Keith Langston

PEN & SWORD
TRANSPORT

First published in Great Britain in 2019 by
Pen & Sword Transport
An imprint of
Pen & Sword Books Ltd
47 Church Street
Barnsley
South Yorkshire
S70 2AS

ISBN 978 1 52675 982 5

A CIP catalogue record for this book is
available from the British Library.

Typeset in 11pt Minion by Mac Style
Printed and bound in India by Replika Press Pvt. Ltd.

Pen & Sword Books Limited incorporates the imprints of Atlas,
Archaeology, Aviation, Discovery, Family History, Fiction, History, Maritime, Military,
Military Classics, Politics, Select, Transport, True Crime, Air World, Frontline Publishing,
Leo Cooper, Remember When, Seaforth Publishing, The Praetorian Press, Wharncliffe Local
History, Wharncliffe Transport, Wharncliffe True Crime and White Owl.

For a complete list of Pen & Sword titles please contact
PEN & SWORD BOOKS LIMITED
47 Church Street, Barnsley, South Yorkshire, S70 2AS, England
E-mail: enquiries@pen-and-sword.co.uk
Website: www.pen-and-sword.co.uk

CONTENTS

A selection of QR codes are listed which when scanned with a hand-held device open appropriate film clips.

'A4' class locomotive DWIGHT D. EISENHOWER moves into the National Railway Museum's Great Hall.

TORNADO on the mainline – Scotland 2013.

'D11' class BUTLER HENDERSON seen in 2007.

'J36' class MAUDE at Bo'ness in 2014.

'D40' class GORDON HIGHLANDER.

Great Central '9P' 4-6-0 No 1165 VALOUR is seen circa 1922. The GC '9P' class was re-classified 'B3' class by the LNER, this locomotive becoming No 6165. *Rail Photoprints Collection*

Gresley 'A4' Pacific BR No 60008 DWIGHT D. EISENHOWER is seen passing Finsbury Park signal box on 5 August 1955 with 'The Flying Scotsman'. BKB Green/ *Norman Preedy Collection*

Chapter 1

INTRODUCTION

LNER locomotive 'J36' class 0-6-0 BR No 65236 HORNE seen with the name painted on to the centre wheel splasher with a cast maker's plate mounted below. This Cowlairs Works built locomotive was one of 123 engines of this class introduced un-named between 1888 and 1900, which later came into BR stock. After the end of World War I some of the class received military associated names. *Norman Preedy Collection*

Naming

The naming of steam locomotives in particular, and other railway locomotives and rolling stock in general has been an accepted practice since the very first railway locomotives appeared in 1804. The practice can fairly be said to be a 'very British tradition'. Numbers were also used to identify individual locomotives, although interestingly the Great Western Railway (GWR) Swindon-built 'Broad Gauge' locomotives at first carried only names.

The relevant locomotive classes concerned are of importance in that they represent the amazing engineering achievements of an industry now long gone, which in its time employed literally thousands of people. Accordingly, the names of aircraft and naval vessels are a tribute to the workers who built them, often in the most testing of circumstances. The chosen locomotive names are a tribute to the military personnel and citizens of our country, commonwealth and allies who lost their lives in conflicts.

Locomotive names have been inspired by a wide variety of topics and those connected with the military have figured prominently. This publication highlights steam locomotives given names with a military connection and originally built/ designed by the London & North Eastern Railway (LNER) or their constituent companies, which then came into British Railways (BR) stock in 1948.

The people who chose and bestowed locomotive names obviously thought it significantly important to do so, and as such those names and their origins are worthy of investigation and explanation. We must take into account that choices made so many years ago, may not have obvious rationale when judged using 21st century ideals. The majority of name choice origins highlighted are obvious in having been conferred to mark significant historic events, military groups, prominent personnel, battles and machines of war etc. However, all are interesting and in their individual ways help to provide snapshots of Britain's military and social history.

After a railway company had decided to allocate names to some of its locomotives, suggestions – often within a predetermined category – were then made by that company's officials and/or other interested parties. Not all of those choices necessarily met with complete approval, and whilst some were rejected others were accepted and indeed occasionally modified after further discussion. Where names were chosen by committees it is good to remember the old maxim 'A camel is a horse, designed by a committee'. However, the choices of military names were less contentious and therefore easier to define.

Constraints did of course apply and those mainly related to the style and size of nameplate and accordingly the amount of space available for the lettering etc. Cast metal nameplates became the accepted practice in most instances, with those being placed one either side of the locomotive concerned often on wheel splashers, smoke deflectors or fixed directly to the boiler cladding or running plate.

However, within the LNER there were notable exceptions in that the name was simply painted onto a wheel splasher. Designated regions of the company adopted differing ways of carrying names, even on locomotives of the same class. For example, Scottish based 4-4-0 'D11' class locomotives had their names painted on the wheel splasher whilst the English based members of the class carried a cast nameplate which was attached to the wheel splasher.

Whilst the Southern Railway, London Midland & Scottish Railway and to a lesser degree the Great Western Railway gave complete classes (or large sections of them) names with military connections, the London & North Eastern Railway did not. Whilst the majority of the highlighted locomotive names in this book were bestowed ex-works, others were either given later in the locomotive's working life, or resulted from a name change. Locomotives included are for the main part those which came into British Railways (BR) stock in 1948, or others outside that remit but of significant importance. For primary identification BR numbers (where applicable) are used, and in the listings preserved locomotives are identified by the letter **P**.

A1 Trust Peppercorn Pacific No 60163 TORNADO is seen passing Brinkworth with 'The Cathedrals Express' London Victoria–Swansea 1Z88 working on St. David's Day, 1 March 2010. *Craig Tiley*

Chapter 2

LONDON & NORTH EASTERN RAILWAY/BRITISH RAILWAYS EASTERN REGION – SCOTTISH REGION

The London & North Eastern Railway (LNER) was formed during the railway period referred to as 'Grouping', as detailed in the *Railways Act 1921* and which took effect on 1 January 1923. Many classes of locomotives included in the original listing subsequently came into British Railways stock in 1948.

Principal members of the 1923 LNER grouping included:
Great Central Railway (GCR)
Great Eastern Railway (GER)
Great North of Scotland Railway (GNoSR)
Great Northern Railway (GNR)
Hull & Barnsley Railway (HBR)
Lancashire, Derbyshire & East Coast Railway (LDECR)
Metropolitan Railway (Met)
Midland & Great Northern Joint Railway (M&GNJR)
Manchester, Sheffield & Lincolnshire Railway (MSLR)
North British Railway (NBR)
North Eastern Railway (NER)

LNER Crest.

Numerically the ex LNER Group BR locomotives carried numbers in the series 60000 to 69999.
A total of 6,418 steam locomotives surviving from that grouping were listed in the December 1948 BR stock list.

1948

British Railways (BR), which from 1965 traded as British Rail, was the state-owned company that operated most of the rail transport in Great Britain between 1948 and 1997. It was formed from the nationalisation of the so-called 'Big Four' British railway companies (LMS, LNER, GWR, SR) and lasted until the gradual privatisation of British Rail, in stages between 1994 and 1997. Originally a trading brand of the Railway Executive of the British Transport Commission, it became an independent statutory corporation in 1962 designated as the British Railways Board.

At the onset of nationalisation locomotive tenders carried no logo but instead the name British Railways. Ex GCR 4-4-0 'D11' class Large Director BR No 62670 MARNE is seen at Lincoln Station in June 1949. *RCTS Archive*

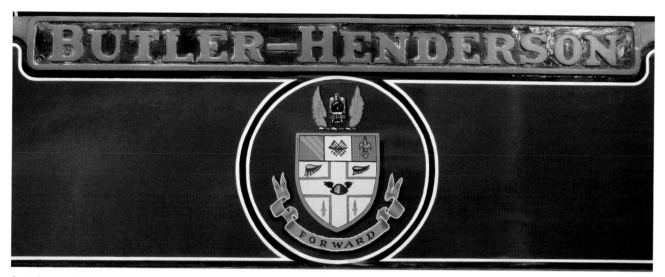

Great Central Railway crest as applied to preserved 'D11' class locomotive BR No 61660 BUTLER-HENDERSON, which in 2019 was based at the Great Central Railway, Loughborough. *Len Mills*

Two differing styles of North Eastern Railway crests. *Keith Langston Collection*

'Lion on a Bike' (cycling lion) emblem from 1950. *Keith Langston Collection*

'Ferret & Dartboard' crest used 1956 onwards. *Keith Langston Collection*

The North British Railway Company crest. *Len Mills*

Great Eastern Railway heraldic device incorporated in a gate at Liverpool Street Station. Shields clockwise from 1 o'clock: Maldon, Ipswich, Norwich, Cambridge, Hertford, Northampton, Huntingdon and Middlesex. Centre: City of London. *Len Mills*

Robinson 'B3' 4P 4-6-0s (originally Great Central Railway '9P' class) commonly known as the 'Lord Faringdon' class.

Gorton Works built 6 of the 4-cylinder locomotives between 1917 and 1920, and they were Robinson's largest class of 4-6-0s. They were fast and powerful engines but on the downside tended to burn large amounts of coal. In an effort to improve their efficiency Gresley rebuilt 4 of the 'B3' class with Caprotti valve gear, LNER Nos 6166, 6168 in 1929, 6164 in 1939 and 6167 in 1938. Those locomotives were reclassified B3/2 and after being fitted with that particular type of valve gear, an average coal saving of 16 per cent was reported.

In 1943 Thompson concluded that the type could be similar to his 'B1' class if rebuilt, accordingly LNER No 6166 EARL HAIG was chosen. It was completely rebuilt becoming a 2-cylinder engine with a high running plate, being reclassified B3/3. However, the locomotive regularly suffered from cracked frames and as a consequence all further rebuilds were cancelled. Although none of the express passenger locomotives were actually operational during the British Railways era, one of the class LNER No 6166 EARL HAIG was allocated the BR number 61497 in April 1948.

In addition to the aforementioned BR No 61497, there is sufficient reason to include details of 3 of the class in a 'Military Connections' listing. For example, although never becoming a BR locomotive 'B3' engine LNER No 6165 (1496) carried the name VALOUR, bestowed '**In memory of G C R EMPLOYEES WHO GAVE THEIR LIVES FOR THEIR COUNTRY 1914–1918**'.

Even though the Great Central Railway ceased to exist after railway 'Grouping' and with the benefit of hindsight, was it perhaps remiss of the London & North Eastern Railway not to transfer the commemorative name to another locomotive? After all, the London & North Western Railway famous PATRIOT continued in use after that company's demise, albeit on a London Midland & Scottish Railway locomotive. Three of the class carried military related names but the other three did not, those being named LORD FARINGDON, LLOYD GEORGE and LORD STUART OF WORTLEY respectively.

VALOUR nameplate. *Len Mills*

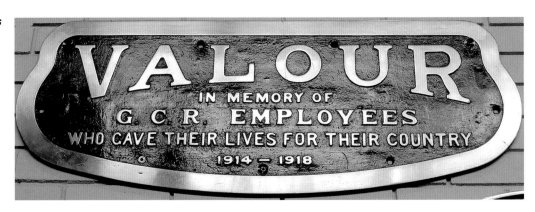

Robinson 'B3' class LNER No 6165 VALOUR is seen with a full tender of coal in 1936, at a location believed to be Neasden. Note the nameplate fixed centrally to the driving wheel splasher. With the 4-6-0 wheel arrangement, Belpaire firebox, long parallel boiler and 6ft 9 ins diameter driving wheels, the Robinson 'B3' looks to be every inch an express passenger engine. *Rail Photoprints Collection*

GCR No 1164 EARL BEATTY, (LNER 6164 and 1495) built at Gorton Works, Manchester, the locomotive entered traffic June 1920 and became an LNER engine at 'Grouping'. It was rebuilt as B3/2 (Caprotti valve gear) in June 1939. Withdrawn from Immingham depot and cut up by the LNER in September 1947.

LMS Stanier 'Jubilee' class BR No 45677 carried the name BEATTY.

Ex-Great Central Railway '9P' class 4-6-0 which became LNER 'B3' class is seen as LNER No 6164 EARL BEATTY at Lincoln in June 1937. *Rail Photoprints Collection*

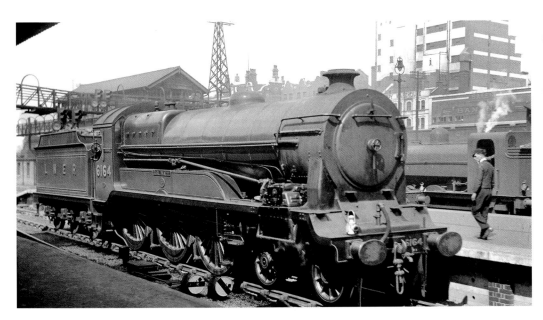

LNER 'B3/2' class LNER No 6164 EARL BEATTY is seen at Kings Cross station in August 1939 shortly after being converted to a Caprotti valve gear locomotive. Note the Ex-Great North Railway 'J52' class 0-6-0ST standing at the adjacent platform whilst on station pilot duties. *Rail Photoprints Collection*

David Richard Beatty, GCB, OM, GCVO, DSO, PC

Admiral of the Fleet 1st Earl Beatty was born in Stapeley, Nantwich Cheshire on 17 January 1871. He was the second son born to army Captain David Longfield Beatty. He was educated at Kilkenny College and thereafter at the Burney's Naval Academy, Gosport (1882). Beatty joined the Royal Navy in 1884, he was promoted to lieutenant in August 1892, and then to captain in 1900. In 1910 Alfred Winsloe, Fourth Sea Lord requested that Beatty be promoted to Rear Admiral even though he had not completed the requisite time as a captain. In 1912 he was appointed Naval Secretary by the then First Lord of the Admiralty Winston Churchill.

Beatty became Rear Admiral in March 1913, Vice Admiral in February 1915, full Admiral in January 1919 and Admiral of the Fleet in May 1919. Beatty was created 1st Earl Beatty, Viscount Borodale and Baron Beatty of the North Sea and Brooksby in October 1919. Beatty died on 12 March 1936 in London. His coffin was draped in the Union Flag flown by his flagship *HMS Queen Elizabeth* in 1919. Beatty is buried at St Paul's Cathedral.

Vice Admiral Sir David Beatty seen in 1916. *John Buchan*

LNER 'B3' 4-6-0 No 6164 EARL BEATTY, at an unidentified location circa 1946. *SA Archive/Rail Photoprints*

GCR No 1165 VALOUR, (LNER 6165 and 1496) built at Gorton Works, Manchester, the locomotive entered traffic July 1920 and became an LNER engine at 'Grouping'. Withdrawn from Lincoln depot and cut up by the LNER in December 1947.

LNER 'B3' 4-6-0 No 6165 VALOUR with Stephenson valve gear, is seen at an unidentified Great Central Railway location circa 1934. This locomotive was not rebuilt by the LNER but did appear in 'Apple Green' livery. *Mike Morant Collection*

GCR No 1166 EARL HAIG, (LNER 6166 and 1497) built at Gorton Works, Manchester, the locomotive entered traffic August 1920 and became an LNER engine at 'Grouping'. Rebuilt in December 1929 as a B3/2 and rebuilt again in October 1943 as a B3/3. Allocated BR No 61497 in 1948, withdrawn and cut up by BR in April 1949.

BR Standard 'Britannia' class Pacific No 70044 also carried the name EARL HAIG.

LNER 'B3' 4-6-0 No 6166 EARL HAIG is seen on the turntable at Neasden as a B3/2, Caprotti engine, on 18 February 1939. This locomotive was converted to a B3/3 in October 1943. *Norman Preedy Collection*

Earl Haig, Douglas Haig, 1st Earl Haig, KT, GCB, OM, GCVO, KCIE, ADC, (1861–1928) was a senior British Army officer during World War I. He was born in Edinburgh and his father John Haig, was head of the family whisky distilling business Haig & Haig. Haig was commander of the *British Expeditionary Force (BEF)* from 1915 until the end of the war.

He was commander during the *Battle of the Somme* where the British Army suffered the highest number of battle casualties ever in military history. Although he had gained a favourable reputation during the immediate post-war years, with his funeral becoming a day of national mourning, Haig has, since the 1960s, become an object of criticism for his leadership during the First World War. Haig went on to command the army during the *Third Battle of Ypres* and the *Hundred Days Offensive* which followed. In that action he led the BEF when it crossed the Canal du Nord and broke through the Hindenburg line, capturing 195,000 German prisoners.

This campaign, in combination with the Kiel mutiny, the Wilhelmshaven mutiny, the proclamation of a republic on 9 November 1918, and civil unrest across Germany, led to the armistice of 11 November 1918. It is considered by some historians to be one of the greatest victories ever achieved by a British-led army.

The 'Earl Haig Fund' launched post World War I, which led to poppies being made and sold in Scotland was effectively the forerunner of the modern-day tradition of wearing poppies on 'Remembrance Day' now administered by the British Legion. Haig is buried at Dryburgh Abbey on the Scottish borders.

Earl Haig statue, Edinburgh Castle. The statue was commissioned by Sir Dhunjibhoy Bomanji of Bombay (now Mumbai). It was once in full public view near the Castle entrance, but is now relatively hidden away in a back courtyard at the entrance to the National War Museum. *Kim Traynor*

LNER Gresley 'A4' class 'Streamlined' Pacific – Classified 7P, re-classified 8P in 1951

The LNER Doncaster works plate as attached to preserved 'A4' locomotive BR No 60008 DWIGHT D. EISENHOWER. (as built GOLDEN SHUTTLE). *Phil Brown*

Of all the London & North Eastern Railways (LNER) Pacific locomotives the Gresley 'A4' class streamlined engines were certainly amongst the most popular with both rail travellers and railway enthusiasts. In the early 1930s the management of the LNER were well aware of the competition for the then lucrative Anglo Scottish and Yorkshire/North Eastern passenger business. To help compete, and hopefully increase their market share, the LNER board identified three important factors which were speed, passenger comfort and reliability.

The LNER was in direct competition with their old rival the London Midland & Scottish Railway (LMS). Under their then newly appointed Chief Mechanical Engineer (CME) William A. Stanier the LMS in 1933 introduced a new class of Pacific locomotives, specifically the 'Princess Royal' class which was introduced to capture a bigger share of the Anglo Scottish passenger business. LNER Chief Mechanical Engineer (CME) Nigel Gresley (later Sir Nigel Gresley) was well aware of the task in hand.

Other countries had already embraced streamlining. In Germany the diesel-electric powered 'Fliegende Hamburger' (Flying Hamburger) had been put into service in 1933 with a timetable that required long stretches being travelled at 85mph. In the United States the 'Burlington Zephyr' reportedly travelled at speeds of 112.5mph during its 1015-mile scheduled run. Whilst in France Gresley had seen a wedge-shaped Bugatti design of railcar and that was said to be the inspiration for the exterior appearance of the 'A4' class. Gresley also went to Germany specifically to travel on the 'Flying Hamburger' and he was said to have been impressed by the use of streamlining, instantly realising its advantage at high speeds.

The first of the new 3-cylinder locomotives LNER No 2509 SILVER KING (BR No 60016) was completed at Doncaster Works in September 1935, 34 of the class were introduced by the end of 1938. The look of the locomotive took the railway world by surprise, it was by the standard of those times different, to say the very least. The Gresley 'A4' class was in steam engineering terms a development of the 'A3' class but it could not possibly have looked more dissimilar.

Whilst the streamlined 'A4' design is synonymous with the Gresley name it must be said that the choice of streamlining for the new design was firmly championed by Sir Ralph Wedgwood, the LNER company chairman at that time. He was supported in that regard by the input of Gresley's assistant, Oliver Vaughan Snell Bulleid an engineer who would later play his own part in the streamlined locomotive story. As built the 'A4' class engines were fitted with valences (side skirting) over the driving wheels but during the war years they were removed to simplify maintenance. To facilitate crew changes on non-stop runs most of the class were coupled to corridor tenders.

Gresley 'A4' class Pacific LNER No 4496 (BR No 60008) is seen as originally named GOLDEN SHUTTLE whilst passing Eryholme, North Yorkshire with an up express, circa 1938. The locomotive was renamed DWIGHT D EISENHOWER on 25 September 1945. Note the valence (side skirting) covering the driving wheels. The locomotive had LNER Silver and Grey livery. *Chris Davies Collection/Rail Photoprints*

Four of the class were built with Kylchap blast-pipes and double chimneys which by all accounts improved their running characteristics at high speeds, all of the others were built with single chimneys. Some of the class were attached to corridor tenders in order to allow a change of locomotive crew during long non-stop runs. British Railways (BR) later rebuilt the whole of the class as double chimney engines.

The 'A4' Pacifics became regarded as Gresley's masterpiece and they surely proved that when No 4468 MALLARD (BR 60022) broke the World speed record for steam locomotives. On 7 July 1938 a speed of 126 mph was reportedly reached on Stoke Bank, and that occasion has been well documented. Gresley was never entirely happy with the 126mph timing and expressed an opinion that it was 'misleading' in the event the LNER claimed a peak average of 125mph and that was enough to beat the German held record speed of 124.5 mph. However, the commemorative plaque fixed upon the locomotive shows the record speed as 126mph.

Only one member of the class was bestowed with a name directly connected to the military, that locomotive is a preserved example BR No 60008 DWIGHT D. EISENHOWER. However, several other locomotives carried less obvious but noteworthy military connected names. In all cases the 'A4' nameplates were carried on the boiler cladding either side of the smokebox.

Dr. Sir Herbert Nigel Gresley C.B.E. – Great Northern Railway/London North Eastern Railway

Although his family was from Netherseal, Derbyshire Herbert Nigel Gresley was actually born in Edinburgh on 19 June 1876. Gresley was educated at a school in Sussex and thereafter at Marlborough College (1890–1893). After leaving college Gresley joined the London & North Western Railway (LNWR) at Crewe Works where he was an apprentice under F.W. Webb. On the completion of his indentures, in 1897 he became employed by the company and worked on the shop floor for a year.

Gresley moved to the Lancashire & Yorkshire Railway (L&YR) in 1898 where he worked under the engineer J.A.F. Aspinall. At the L&YR he served at the Blackpool depot as foreman of the running sheds and also worked in the L&YR Carriage & Wagon Department. Gresley left to join the Great Northern Railway (GNR) in 1905, in order to take up the post of Superintendent in the Carriage & Wagon Department. In 1911 he was appointed Chief Mechanical Engineer (CME) of the GNR. Following 'Grouping' Gresley was appointed to the post of CME with the London North Eastern Railway (LNER).

Gresley was awarded the C.B.E. in 1920, knighted in 1936 and made an honorary Doctor of Science by Manchester University in that same year.

Dr. Sir Herbert Nigel Gresley C.B.E. died at his Hertfordshire home on 5 April after a short illness.

60001 SIR RONALD MATTHEWS (LNER 4500, 1 – 1946 number) built at Doncaster Works, Order No 342 – Works No 1873. Entered traffic in April 1938 named GARGANEY, renamed March 1939. Withdrawn by BR in October 1964 and cut up in January 1965 by Hughes Bolckows, North Blyth.

Gresley 'A4' class Pacific BR No 60001 SIR RONALD MATTHEWS hurries through Portobello East Junction (ECML) on 27 August 1962. The locomotive had BR Brunswick Green, orange and black lined livery. *RCTS Archive*

Gresley 'A4' class Pacific LNER No 4500 SIR RONALD MATTHEWS is seen at Grantham, when newly named in April 1939 (previously named GARGANEY). This locomotive became BR No 60001. Note the tender markings and the valence (side skirting) covering the driving wheels. The locomotive had LNER Garter Blue, narrow red and white lined livery. *Rail Photoprints Collection*

Gresley 'A4' class Pacific BR No 60001 SIR RONALD MATTHEWS is seen ex works condition at Doncaster, during 1957. The locomotive had BR Brunswick Green, orange and black lined livery. *G.B. Wallis/Rail Photoprints*

Gresley 'A4' class Pacific BR No 60001 SIR RONALD MATTHEWS is pictured climbing to Stoke Tunnel with an up express, circa 1959. The locomotive had BR Brunswick Green, orange and black lined livery. *Rail Photoprints Collection*

Sir Ronald Wilfred Matthews, was born on 25 June 1885 in Sheffield, England, Matthews was a prominent steel manufacturer and conservative politician. He was a student of Eton College, and also studied in Switzerland and Germany. He was Master Cutler, Sheffield, 1922–1923 who served as Chairman of the London & North Eastern Railway (LNER) between 1938–1948. Matthews was a captain in King's Own Yorkshire Light Infantry, 1914–1918. He was also a member of the Inland Transport War Council, 1941–1945.

The King's Own Yorkshire Light Infantry (KOYLI) was a light infantry regiment of the British Army. It officially existed from 1881 to 1968, but its predecessors go back to 1755. In 1968, the regiment was amalgamated with the Somerset and Cornwall Light Infantry, the King's Shropshire Light Infantry and the Durham Light Infantry to form The Light Infantry, which in turn was merged with the Devonshire and Dorset Regiment, the Royal Gloucestershire, Berkshire and Wiltshire Regiment and the Royal Green Jackets to become The Rifles in 2007.

Cap badge of 'KOYLI', with hunting horn, white rose and crown.

60002 SIR MURROUGH WILSON (LNER 4499, 2 – 1946 number) built at Doncaster Works, Order No 342 – Works No 1872. Entered traffic in April 1938 named POCHARD, renamed April 1939. Withdrawn by BR in May 1964 and cut up in July 1964 by Cohens, Cargo Fleet.

Gresley 'A4' class Pacific BR No 60002 SIR MURROUGH WILSON is seen at Darlington station whilst heading a morning cross-country service, in this 1963 image. The locomotive had BR Brunswick Green, orange and black lined livery. *Mike Morant Collection*

Gresley 'A4' class Pacific BR No 60002 SIR MURROUGH WILSON pictured during a March 1959 visit to Doncaster Works after receiving a new boiler and whilst having 'AWS' fitted. *Rail Photoprints Collection*

Lieutenant-Colonel Sir Murrough John Wilson KBE (14 September 1875–20 April 1946) was a British Army officer, member of parliament, and railway executive. He served as the Unionist MP for Richmond (Yorkshire) from 1918 to 1929. Wilson was born at Cliffe Hall, on the southern bank of the River Tees, County Durham in what is now the district of Richmondshire, North Yorkshire. His father, Col. John Gerald Wilson CB, was an officer in the York and Lancaster Regiment, and died of wounds during the Boer War, at Tweebosch. Murrough Wilson was one of seven children, and the second-oldest of four brothers. The oldest brother, Lt. Richard Bassett Wilson, was also killed in the Boer War, at Rustenburg. The third brother, Lt.-Col. Denis Daly Wilson MC, was killed in action in France during the First World War, while the fourth brother, Capt. Sir Frank O'Brien Wilson, was a Royal Navy officer.

After completing his education at Marlborough College, Wilson joined the North Eastern Railway (NER) in 1893, and in 1912 was appointed a director of the company. An officer with the 2nd/5th Battalion of the West Yorkshire Regiment during the First World War, he was elected to parliament at the 1918 general election. Maintaining his directorship of the NER throughout the war Wilson continued as a director after the formation of the London and North Eastern Railway (LNER) in 1923. From 1924, he was also chairman of the Navy, Army and Air Force Institutes (NAAFI), for which he

NER crest on the former headquarters building of the railway, Station Rise, York. It shows three constituent companies amalgamated in 1854. They are – Top, York & North Midland Railway. Left, Leeds Northern Railway. Right, York Newcastle & Berwick Railway. *Len Mills*

NAAFI motto; Latin *Servitor Servientium*, translated as The Servants.

was knighted in 1927. Wilson was a Deputy Lieutenant of the North Riding of Yorkshire in later life, and held various directorships. He succeeded his father as lord of Cliffe Hall, and died there in 1946, aged 70.

The Yorkshire Regiment (14th/15th, 19th and 33rd/76th Foot) (abbreviated YORKS) is an infantry regiment of the British Army, created by the amalgamation of three historic regiments in 2006. It is currently the only line infantry or rifles unit to represent a single geographical county in the new infantry structure, serving as the county regiment of Yorkshire. It lost one battalion as part of the Army 2020 defence review.

The Navy, Army and Air Force Institutes (NAAFI) is an organisation created by the Government in 1921 to run recreational establishments needed by the British Armed Forces, and to sell goods to servicemen and their families. NAAFI's greatest contribution was during the Second World War. By April 1944 the NAAFI ran 7,000 canteens and had 96,000 personnel (expanded from fewer than 600 canteens and 4,000 personnel in 1939). At start of the Second World War it was said to have the biggest pantry in the world.

Honorary Colours of the Yorkshire Regiment being paraded through York in September 2007. *Richard Harvey*

60004 SIR WILLIAM WHITELAW (LNER 4462, 4 – 1946 number) built at Doncaster Works, Order No 341A – Works No 1864. Entered traffic in November 1937 named GREAT SNIPE, renamed July 1941. Withdrawn by BR in July 1966 and cut up in December 1966 by Motherwell Machinery & Scrap, Wishaw.

Gresley 'A3' class Pacific LNER No 2563 (became BR 60064) carried the name WILLIAM WHITELAW until 1941.

Gresley 'A4' class Pacific BR No 60004 WILLIAM WHITELAW seen approaching Edinburgh Waverley station, as it passes through Princes Street Gardens with an Aberdeen–Edinburgh service, in 1956. Note the double chimney. The locomotive had BR Brunswick Green, orange and black lined livery. *Rail Photoprints Collection*

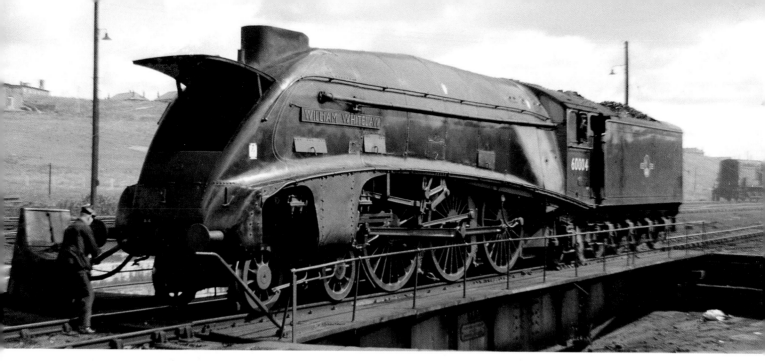

Gresley 'A4' class Pacific BR No 60004 WILLIAM WHITELAW seen on the turntable at Perth, during 1962. The locomotive had BR Brunswick Green, orange and black lined livery. *Martyn Hunt/Rail Photoprints*

William Stephen Ian Whitelaw, 1st Viscount Whitelaw, KT, CH, MC, PC, DL (28 June 1918–1 July 1999), often known as Willie Whitelaw, was a British Conservative Party politician who served in a wide number of Cabinet positions, most notably as Home Secretary and de facto Deputy Prime Minister. Whitelaw was born at the family home in Nairn in northeast Scotland. He was educated at Wixenford School, Wokingham, before passing the entrance exam to Winchester College and thence to Trinity College, Cambridge, where he won a blue for golf and joined the Officer Training Corps. By chance he was in a summer camp in 1939 on the outbreak of the Second World War and was granted a regular, not wartime, commission in the British Army, in the Scots Guards.

Insignia of the 6th Guards Tank Brigade.

Whitelaw later served in the 6th Guards Tank Brigade. He commanded Churchill tanks in Normandy during the Second World War and during Operation Bluecoat in late July 1944. His unit was the first Allied to encounter German 'Jagdpanther' tank destroyers, being attacked by three of them. During that action the battalion's second-in-command was killed when his tank was hit by enemy fire. Whitelaw succeeded to that position, holding it, with the rank of Major, throughout the advance through the Netherlands into Germany and until the end of the war. He was awarded the Military Cross for his actions at Caumont. After the end of the war in Europe, Whitelaw's unit was posted to Palestine. He left the army in 1946 to take care of the family estates of Gartshore and Woodhall in Lanarkshire. During his retirement and until his death, Lord Whitelaw was the chairman of the board of Governors at St Bees School, Cumbria. He was appointed a Knight of the Thistle in 1990. He died aged 81, in July 1999, he was buried at St. Andrew's Parish Church, Dacre, Cumbria.

Churchill tanks of 6th Guards Tank Brigade laying a smokescreen during the advance on Venray, Netherlands, 17 October 1944. *Sgt. Hewitt No 5 Army Film and Photographic Unit*

60006 SIR RALPH WEDGWOOD (LNER 4469) built at Doncaster Works, Order No 342 – Works No 1868. Entered traffic in January 1938 named GADWALL, renamed March 1941. In April 1942 the locomotive was withdrawn and scrapped by the LNER following damage sustained during a bombing raid. The number and name were transferred to LNER No 4466 HERRING GULL (1946 number 6). It was withdrawn by BR in September 1965 and cut up in October 1966 by Motherwell Machinery & Scrap, Wishaw.

Sir Ralph Lewis Wedgwood, 1st Baronet CB CMG (2 March 1874– 5 September 1956)

He was chairman of the wartime Railway Executive Committee from September 1939 to August 1941. He served sixteen years as Chief Officer of the LNER (1923 and 1939).

LNER engine No 4469 was named SIR RALPH WEDGWOOD in March 1939.

That 'A4' class locomotive was stabled at York North Shed on the night of 28/29 April 1942, the occasion of the 'Baedeker Raid' on York. During the attack, York station and North Shed were bombed.

The 'A4' Pacific and another nearby engine, 'B16' class LNER No 925 were damaged after a bomb fell through the shed roof and exploded between the two engines. The Gresley locomotive was severely damaged as a result of the explosion, but was recovered and towed to Doncaster shortly afterward. Due to the degree of damage, it was considered impractical to rebuild No 4469, and the locomotive was condemned and later scrapped.

Gresley 'A4' class Pacific BR No 60006 SIR RALPH WEDGEWOOD at the Kings Cross bufferstops after arrival with the up 'Flying Scotsman' on 29 May 1953. The locomotive had BR Brunswick Green, orange and black lined livery. The locomotive carries two headboards the 'Flying Scotsman' and also one commemorating the Coronation of Queen Elizabeth II. *Rail Photoprints Collection*

Gresley 'A4' class Pacific BR No 60006 SIR RALPH WEDGEWOOD lays down a heavy plume of smoke as it passes a freight train, whilst heading an up express near Little Ponton, circa 1950. *Rail Photoprints Collection*

60008 DWIGHT D. EISENHOWER (LNER 4496, 8 – 1946 number) built at Doncaster Works, Order No 341 – Works No 1861. Entered traffic in September 1937 named GOLDEN SHUTTLE, renamed September 1945. Withdrawn by BR in July 1963 and saved for preservation. **P** Normally based at the National Railroad Museum of USA.

Preserved Gresley 'A4' class Pacific BR No 60008 DWIGHT D. EISENHOWER on display at the National Railway Museum, York in 2013. *Phil Brown*

The locomotive was transported by sea to the USA, it arrived in New York on 11 May 1964 and was then transported by rail to the aforementioned museum. Notably it was moved to Abilene, Kansas for the celebrations of the centenary of Eisenhower's birth in October 1990. The move both ways was done as a special train movement at slow speed, since the locomotive and two cars from the command train used the British vacuum braking system which is incompatible with modern day American air-braked trains. Two restored British passenger carriages, which were once used as part of Eisenhower's Command Train are normally displayed with the locomotive.

In 2012, the National Railway Museum (NRM) announced plans to temporarily repatriate the engine from its American location, as part of a plan to reunite all six preserved 'A4' locomotives for the 75th anniversary of the class's world record breaking 126 mph run. Accordingly, 'A4' BR No 60008 was loaned to the National Railway Museum, York for a period of two years. Whilst at the NRM the locomotive was once again cosmetically overhauled, and received a new livery of authentic BR Brunswick Green, orange and black lining. The background colour on the Dwight D. Eisenhower nameplates was also changed from red to black. The locomotive returned to America in early 2014.

BR No 60008 DWIGHT D. EISENHOWER was withdrawn from service on 20 July 1963. Earmarked for the National Railroad Museum in Green Bay, Wisconsin USA. Prior to shipping the locomotive was cosmetically restored at Doncaster Works, in July 1963. *Phil Brown*

Dwight David 'Ike' Eisenhower (14 October 1890–28 March 1969)
Born David Dwight Eisenhower in Denison, Texas, he was raised in Kansas in a large family of mostly Pennsylvania Dutch ancestry.

He was an American army general and statesman who served as the 34th president of the United States from 1953 to 1961. He graduated from West Point in 1915 and during World War I, he was denied a request to serve in Europe and instead commanded a unit that trained tank crews. Following the war, he served under various generals and was promoted to the rank of brigadier general in 1941. During World War II, he was a five-star general in the United States Army and served as supreme commander of the Allied Expeditionary Forces in Europe. He was responsible for planning and supervising the invasion of North Africa in Operation Torch in 1942–43 and the successful invasion of France and Germany in 1944–45 from the Western Front. After the war, Eisenhower served as Army Chief of Staff and in 1951–52, he served as the first Supreme Commander of NATO. President Eisenhower died on 28 March 1969 and was interred in a small chapel in the grounds of the Eisenhower Presidential Library at Abilene, Kansas on 2 April 1969.

Eisenhower as General of the Army. *US Army Signal Corps*

Gresley 'A4' class Pacific BR No 60008 DWIGHT D. EISENHOWER prepares to leave Peterborough, on 9 April 1961. The locomotive had BR Brunswick Green, orange and black lined livery. *Rail Photoprints Collection*

Gresley 'A4' class Pacific BR No 60008 DWIGHT D. EISENHOWER is seen departing from Kings Cross Station with an express passenger train for Newcastle on Saturday 28 February 1959. The locomotive had BR Brunswick Green, orange and black lined livery. *J & J Collection – Sid Rickard/Rail Photoprints*

Gresley 'A4' class Pacific BR No 60008 DWIGHT D. EISENHOWER seen leaving Grantham with an up express for Kings Cross, circa 1958. *Rail Photoprints Collection*

60026 MILES BEEVOR (LNER 4485, 26 – 1946 number) built at Doncaster Works, Order No 340 – Works No 1850. Entered traffic in February 1937 named KESTREL, renamed during a work visit between September and November 1947. Withdrawn by BR in December 1966 and cut up by Hughes Bolckows, North Blyth in September 1967.

Gresley 'A4' class Pacific LNER No 26 KESTREL, earlier LNER No 4485 (later BR No 60026 MILES BEEVOR) is seen with a 16-coach load in the region of Hadley Common. In order to get an approximate date on which this image was taken it is appropriate to note that the locomotive carried No 26 and wartime black livery between 26 May 1946 and 19 September 1947. *Mike Morant Collection*

Miles Beevor (8 March 1900–9 September 1994), was a solicitor, pilot (RAFVR) and businessman.

He was educated at Winchester College, and graduated from New College, Oxford University in 1921 with a Bachelor of Arts degree. He qualified as a solicitor in 1925, and latterly held the office of Justice of the Peace for Hertfordshire.

At the outbreak of World War II, he joined the Royal Air Force Volunteer Reserve and gained the rank of Flight Lieutenant in 1941. He became chief legal advisor for London and North Eastern Railway (LNER) in 1943, a post he held until the LNER was nationalised. On 1 November 1947, just before nationalisation, the company named locomotive No 4485 after him in light of his service.

Beevor was acting Chief General Manager for the LNER in June 1947, after which he became Chief Secretary and legal advisor for the British Transport Commission between 1947 and 1951. Beevor was Managing Director of Brush Group Ltd between 1954 and 1958. Beevor died on 9 September 1994 at the age of 94.

Ensign of the RAF.

Gresley 'A4' class Pacific BR No 60026 MILES BEEVOR is seen as it climbs away from Grantham whilst passing Little Ponton with an up express, in 1948. Note the odd angle of the chime whistle, which appears to have received a hefty knock. Also LNER on the tender. The locomotive had LNER Garter Blue, narrow red and white lined livery. *Rail Photoprints Collection*

Gresley 'A4' class Pacific BR No 60026 MILES BEEVOR, approaching Huntingdon North on 14 March 1959. *Mike Morant Collection*

Gresley 'A4' class Pacific BR No 60026 MILES BEEVOR pauses at Grantham station whilst southbound with a summer service in 1960. Note the near pristine external condition of the 34A Kings Cross allocated engine and the later style BR logo on the tender. In the 1959 and 1960 images the locomotive had BR Brunswick Green, orange and black lined livery. *R.A. Whitfield/Rail Photoprints*

Gresley GNR – LNER 'A3' 7P PACIFIC

In 1922 Gresley introduced the first of his three-cylinder Pacific locomotives to work on the Great Northern Railway (GNR). This class was designed to haul the heaviest loaded and fastest express trains on the GNR and later London North Eastern Railway (LNER) system with the notable exception of the solitary Great Western Railway (GWR) locomotive No 111 GREAT BEAR they were the first 4-6-2 (Pacific) type to be built in Great Britain. This class of 78 engines were built by Doncaster Works (58) and the contractor North British Locomotive Company (20). They were built with larger cabs and for the first time in Britain the enginemen were afforded the luxury of padded seats. To facilitate crew changes on non-stop runs some of the class were coupled to corridor tenders. The class were variously coupled to GNR tenders with coal rails (greedy bars) and also those of LNER design. They were successful in traffic and in addition to one locomotive being a rebuilt GNR 'A10' class, there were five variations to the basic design over their working lives. The popular preserved 'A3' Pacific BR No 60103 FLYING SCOTSMAN was a member of this class. Most of this class were named after famous racehorses but some of those names owed their origin to, or shared a military connection with. The names were carried on curved plates located over the centre driving wheel splasher.

60039 SANDWICH (LNER 2504, 39 – 1946 number) built at Doncaster Works Order No 331 – Works No 1794. Entered traffic in September 1934. Withdrawn by BR in March 1963 and cut up in April 1963 at Doncaster Works.

LMS 'Jubilee' class 4-6-0 BR No 45641 also carried this name.

Sandwich

The 'A3' locomotive was named SANDWICH for a British thoroughbred racehorse that won the classic 'St Leger Stakes' at Doncaster Racecourse in 1931.

The name was shared by six ships of the Royal Navy which were either named for the Kentish seaside town of Sandwich, or one of the holders of the title Earl of Sandwich, particularly Vice-Admiral Edward Montagu, 1st Earl of Sandwich, or First Lord of the Admiralty John Montagu, 4th Earl of Sandwich.

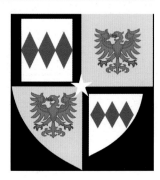

Arms of the Earl of Sandwich.

Gresley 'A3' Pacific BR No 60039 SANDWICH is seen passing Westgate North signal box, Wakefield on 4 August 1956. Note the single chimney and early 'lion on a bike' BR logo on the tender. The locomotive had BR Brunswick Green, orange and black lined livery. *BKB Green/Norman Preedy Collection*

Gresley 'A3' Pacific BR No 60039 SANDWICH is seen on the turntable at Kings Cross motive power depot in 1960, note the LNER tender and the lipped double chimney fitted in July 1959. The locomotive had BR Brunswick Green, orange and black lined livery. *Rail Photoprints Collection*

Gresley 'A3' Pacific BR No 60039 SANDWICH in the shed yard at Gateshead 23 June 1962. Note the German type smoke deflectors which were fitted to this locomotive in March 1962, and also the double chimney. The locomotive had BR Brunswick Green, orange and black lined livery. *Ian Turnbull/Rail Photoprints*

60040 CAMERONIAN (LNER 2505, 575 and 40 – 1946 number) built at Doncaster Works, Order No 331 – Works No 1795. Entered traffic in October 1934. Withdrawn by BR in July 1964 and cut up in the September of that year by Hughes Bolckow, North Blyth.

LMS 'Royal Scot' class 4-6-0 locomotive BR No 46113 also carried this name.

Gresley 'A3' Pacific BR No 60040 CAMERONIAN, awaits its next turn of duty after having been serviced at York depot in the summer of 1950. The 'A3' is in the company of an unidentified member of the same class and NER Worsdell 'D20' BR No 62369. Note the single chimney and GNR tender with post 1948 BRITISH RAILWAYS markings. The locomotive had BR Blue, black and white lined livery. *Rail Photoprints Collection*

The 'A3' locomotive was named CAMERONIAN for a British thoroughbred racehorse that won the '2000 Guineas' and the classic 'Derby' in 1931 and the 'Champion Stakes' in 1932.

The Cameronians (Scottish Rifles) was a rifle regiment of the British Army, the only regiment of rifles amongst the Scottish regiments of infantry. It was formed in 1881 under the Childers Reforms by the amalgamation of the 26th Cameronian Regiment and the 90th Perthshire Light Infantry. In 1968 the regiment chose to be disbanded rather than amalgamated with another regiment, one of only two infantry regiments in the British Army to do so. It could trace its roots to that of the Cameronians, later the 26th of Foot, who were raised in 1689. The 1881 amalgamation coincided with the Cameronians becoming the new Scottish Rifles. After the amalgamation, the 1st Battalion was known as 'Cameronians' while the 2nd was known as 'The Scottish Rifles'.

Cameronians World War II cap badge.

Gresley 'A3' Pacific BR No 60040 CAMERONIAN with lipped double chimney is seen in the shed yard at Darlington depot in May 1960. The locomotive is coupled to a ex GNR tender with coal rails, which has the later BR so called 'ferret and dartboard' logo. Note the Doncaster Works maker's plate mounted on the smoke box and the 'RA9' route availability indication shown on the bottom left cabside panel. The locomotive had BR Brunswick Green, orange and black lined livery. *Norman Preedy Collection*

Route Availability (RA) is the system by which the permanent way and supporting works (bridges, embankments, etc.) of the railway network of Great Britain are graded. All routes are allocated an RA number between 1 and 10. Rolling stock is also allocated an RA (between 1 and 10) and the RA of a train is the highest RA of any of its separate elements. The train must have a route availability (RA) lower than or equal to the RA of a line to be allowed to operate over it. The system was first devised by the London & North Eastern Railway (LNER), and then continued by British Railways (BR).

Cameronians Memorial

This impressive structure commemorates the service of the Cameronians (Scottish Rifles) regiment in the First and Second World Wars. The memorial includes a bronze sculpture representing a machine gun emplacement, with three slightly larger than life size military figures. The memorial was unveiled by Field Marshal Sir Douglas Haig, on 9 August 1924, five days after the tenth anniversary of the outbreak of the war. A plaque for the Second World War was added in 1947.

The sculpture was designed by *Philip Lindsey Clark*. He had enlisted as a private in the Artists' Rifles in 1914, and was commissioned in the 11th (Service) (1st South Down) Battalion of the Royal Sussex Regiment in 1916, ending the war as a captain and being awarded a DSO.

The Cameronians War Memorial is located in Kelvingrove Park, in the west of Glasgow. *Len Mills*

Gresley 'A1' Pacific LNER No 2544 as a newly introduced engine standing outside Doncaster Works in August 1924, and is still awaiting the LEMBERG nameplate. Between 1927 and 1947 all but one of the 'A1' Pacifics were rebuilt and designated 'A3' class.* LEMBERG was amongst the first to be rebuilt towards the end of 1927. The locomotive had LNER Apple Green, black and white lined livery with its number on the GNR railed tender. This locomotive became BR No 60045. *Mike Stokes Archive*

*The exception was LNER No 4470 GREAT NORTHERN which was rebuilt by Thompson in 1945 as class 'A1/1'.

Lemberg

The 'A3' locomotive was named LEMBERG for a British thoroughbred racehorse that won the classic 'Derby' in 1910.

The Battle of Lemberg (Lviv, Lwów) in Polish historiography called the Defence of Lwów, took place from November 1918 to May 1919 and was a six-month long conflict in what is modern-day Ukraine. The battle was fought between attacking forces of the West Ukrainian People's Republic and the local Polish civilian population, assisted later by regular Polish Army forces for the control over the city, in what was then the eastern part of Galicia and now is the western part of Ukraine. The battle sparked the Polish-Ukrainian War, which was ultimately won by Poland.

Gresley 'A3' Pacific BR No 60045 LEMBERG, with lipped double chimney, German style smoke deflectors and a GNR tender with later BR crest is seen at Darlington in 1962. The locomotive had BR Brunswick Green, orange and black lined livery. *Norman Preedy Collection*

Gresley 'A3' Pacific BR No 60045 LEMBERG is attracting the attention of the gricers as it awaits its next turn of duty at Darlington on Saturday 31 July 1965. *Brian Robbins/Rail Photoprints*

Gresley 'A3' Pacific BR No 60045 LEMBERG seen again at Darlington depot in July 1964. In the 1960s images the locomotive had BR Brunswick Green, orange and black lined livery. *Norman Preedy Collection*

60087 BLENHEIM (LNER 2598, 565 and 87 – 1946 number) built at Doncaster Works, Order No 317 – Works No 1743. Entered traffic in June 1930. Withdrawn by BR in October 1963 and cut up in June 1964 by Arnott Young, Carmyle.

The Great Western Railway (GWR) 'Castle' class 4-6-0 locomotive BR No 5073 also carried this name.

Gresley 'A3' Pacific BR No 60087 BLENHEIM approaching Dalmeny station with an Aberdeen service on 23 July 1955. The locomotive had BR Brunswick Green, orange and black lined livery. *David Anderson*

Blenheim

The 'A3' locomotive was named BLENHEIM for a British thoroughbred racehorse that won the classic 'Derby' in 1930.

The Battle of Blenheim, fought on 13 August 1704, was a major battle of the War of the Spanish Succession. The overwhelming Allied victory ensured the safety of Vienna from the Franco-Bavarian army, thus preventing the collapse of the Grand Alliance. Louis XIV of France sought to inflict defeat on the Holy Roman Emperor, Leopold by seizing Vienna, the then Habsburg capital. Vienna was at that time in considerable danger. The Elector of Bavaria and Marshal Marsin's forces in that country threatened from the west. Marshal Vendôme's large army in northern Italy also posed a serious threat, with a potential offensive through the Brenner Pass. Vienna was also under pressure from Rákóczi's Hungarian revolt from the east. The Duke of Marlborough resolved to alleviate the peril to Vienna by marching his forces south from Bedburg and thus support Emperor Leopold within the Grand Alliance. The opposing armies finally met on the banks of the Danube in and around the small village of Blindheim, from which the English 'Blenheim' is derived. Blenheim was one of the battles that altered the course of the war, which until then was leaning in favour of Louis' coalition. France suffered as many as 38,000 casualties and their commander-in-chief, Marshal Tallard, was captured and taken to England.

Memorial for the Battle of Blenheim 1704, Lutzingen, Germany. Translated inscription: War of the Spanish Succession; Battle on 13 August 1704. *Klaus-Dieter Keller*

Gresley 'A3' Pacific BR No 60087 BLENHEIM is seen passing Haymarket shed with the down 'North Briton' for Glasgow Queen Street on 15 October 1953. The locomotive had BR Brunswick Green, orange and black lined livery. *David Anderson*

Blenheim – The Bristol Blenheim was a British light fighter/bomber aircraft designed by Frank Barnwell in 1935. It was built by the Bristol Aeroplane Company and flown by the RAF and allies. The type carried a crew of three airmen, and was one of the first British aircraft to have all-metal stressed-skin, retractable landing gear and flaps, a powered gun turret and variable pitch propellers. The design of the Blenheim proved to be readily adaptable, and was modified to serve in roles such as an interim long-range fighter and as a night fighter.

The aircraft was developed as Type 142, a civil airliner, in response to a challenge from the so called 'press baron' Lord Rothermere to produce the fastest commercial aircraft in Europe. The Type 142 first flew in April 1935, and the Air Ministry, impressed by its performance, ordered a modified design as the Type 142M for the Royal Air Force (RAF) as a bomber. Deliveries of the newly named Blenheim to RAF squadrons commenced on 10 March 1937. There is a preserved example of this aircraft type.

The first production Bristol Blenheim Type 142M with the military serial registration K7033, which served as the only prototype and made its first flight in June 1936. *RAF image*

Gresley 'A3' Pacific BR No 60098 SPION KOP passes Dalmeny with an Aberdeen–Edinburgh Waverley service on 23 July 1955. The single chimney locomotive, with an LNER tender and early BR logo had Brunswick Green, orange and black lined livery. *David Anderson*

Spion Kop

The 'A3' locomotive was named SPION KOP for an Irish-bred British-trained thoroughbred racehorse that won the 1920 'Derby' classic in record time.

This image shows a section of the British graves at the site of the Battle of Spion Kop (Spioenkop). Many of the fallen soldiers were buried in the trenches where they died. These graves therefore give an indication of where the trenches were located at the time of the battle. *Renier Marit*

This gravestone commemorates the British Major General Edward R.P. Woodgate, killed on 24 January 1900 in the Battle of Spioenkop. *NJR ZA*

Spion Kop (or Kop for short) is a colloquial name or term for a number of single tier terraces and stands at sports stadiums, particularly in the United Kingdom. The football terraces' steep nature are said to resemble a hill near Ladysmith, South Africa.

The Battle of Spion Kop was fought about 24-mile (38 km) west-south-west of Ladysmith on the hilltop of Spioenkop along the Tugela River, Natal in South Africa from 23–24 January 1900. It was fought between the South African Republic and the Orange Free State on the one hand and British forces during the Second Boer War campaign to relieve Ladysmith. It resulted in a Boer victory.

Gresley 'A3' Pacific BR No 60098 SPION KOP, the double chimney engine with LNER tender is seen in the shed yard at Haymarket, on 30 December 1960. The locomotive had Brunswick Green, orange and black lined livery. *David Anderson*

Gresley 'A3' Pacific BR No 60098 SPION KOP is seen at Edinburgh Waverley in July 1961. The locomotive had Brunswick Green, orange and black lined livery. Note the two 'Class 26' diesel locomotives one of which, BR No D5302 is preserved and based at the Strathspey Railway. *Norman Preedy Collection*

60107 ROYAL LANCER (LNER 4476, 506 and 107 – 1946 number) built at Doncaster Works, Order No 297 – Works No 1568. Entered traffic in May 1923. Withdrawn by BR in September 1963 and cut up in October 1963 at Doncaster Works.

Gresley 'A3' Pacific BR No 60107 ROYAL LANCER with GNR railed tender is seen preparing to depart from York, in this April 1959 image. This locomotive was fitted with a double chimney in the June of that year. The locomotive had Brunswick Green, orange and black lined livery. *Mike Stokes Archive*

Royal Lancer

The 'A3' locomotive was named ROYAL LANCER for a British thoroughbred racehorse that won both the Doncaster St. Leger and the Curragh Irish St. Leger in 1922.

The 17th Lancers (Duke of Cambridge's Own) was a cavalry regiment of the British Army, raised in 1759 and notable for its participation in the Charge of the Light Brigade during the Crimean War. The regiment was amalgamated with the 21st Lancers to form the 17th/21st Lancers in 1922.

The Royal Lancers is now the last regiment in the British Army to retain the title of lancers. It has directly or indirectly inherited the traditions of the six previous British lancer regiments that were in existence following the Childers Reforms and until a further series of amalgamations began in 1922.

17th Lancers at the Battle of Modderfontein, during the Second Boer War. Fought on 17 September 1901 between a Boer raiding force and a British cavalry squadron led by Captain Sandeman, a cousin of Winston Churchill. 'All that was left of them', a painting by Richard Caton Woodville, Jr. (1856–1927).

Gresley 'A3' Pacific BR No 60107 ROYAL LANCER with German style smoke deflectors is seen during a positioning move at Doncaster station on 25 February 1962. The locomotive had Brunswick Green, orange and black lined livery. *RCTS Archive*

Gresley 'A3' Pacific BR No 60107 ROYAL LANCER in Brunswick Green livery is seen arriving at Grantham with the up 'White Rose' express, on 31 March 1962. 'The White Rose' service operated between Kings Cross and Leeds Central/Bradford Exchange. The initial run took place on 23 May 1949 and the last titled run was on 13 June 1964. Note the 3rd official 'White Rose' head board style, which was used between 30 March and 14 April 1962 only, therefore promoting the 'Wool Wins Campaign' of that time. *Ian Turnbull/Rail Photoprints*

LNER Thompson & Peppercorn Pacific 'A2' class

The 'A2' class were all 3-cylinder locomotives of the Pacific (4-6-2) type and were Mixed Traffic (MT) engines built by Thompson and Peppercorn. However, the 40 strong class was actually made up of 4 very distinct sub-classes (variants). They were introduced by the London & North Eastern Railway (LNER) from 1934 onwards and by British Railways (BR) in 1948, they were built at Darlington and Doncaster Works.

As introduced the various designations were:

'A2/1' a Thompson design of 4 locomotives BR Nos 60507 – 60510, introduced in 1944 and built at Darlington Works. They were originally ordered as 'V2' class 2-6-2 engines but the design was changed and they were built as 4-6-2 types.

'A2/2' introduced in 1943 were Thompson rebuilds from Gresley's 3-cylinder 'P2' class 2-8-2 engines. In total 6 locomotives of this variant, BR Nos 60501–60506 were built at Doncaster works. They differed from the other 'A2' locomotives by not being fitted with conventional type smoke deflectors.

'A2/3' introduced in 1946/47 were actually Thompson's new Pacific design and 15 of those, BR Nos 60511–60524 were built at Doncaster Works during and immediately after his tenure. From 1946 onwards a further 15 were built at Doncaster to a redesign by Peppercorn with a reduced wheel base and single chimneys.

All of the class carried names some of which were re-cycled from withdrawn locomotives etc. In the case of variants with smoke deflectors the names were carried on oblong plates positioned on the deflector plates whilst those without smoke deflectors carried the name on oblong plates positioned either side of the smoke box.

Thompson 'A2/2' BR No 60504. *Norman Preedy Collection*

Where double chimneys were fitted, they were at first of an unlipped style but later chimneys with lips were fitted.

Edward Thompson (25 June 1881–15 July 1954) was an English railway engineer, and was Chief Mechanical Engineer of the London & North Eastern Railway (LNER) between 1941 and 1946. Edward Thompson was born at Marlborough, Wiltshire on 25 June 1881. He was educated at Marlborough before taking the Mechanical Science Tripos at Pembroke College, Cambridge, where he earned a third-class degree. He joined the North Eastern Railway (NER) in 1910 and also worked at the Great Northern Railway (GNR). Thompson retired from the LNER in 1946 and died in 1954.

Arthur Henry Peppercorn, OBE (29 January 1889–3 March 1951) was an English railway engineer, and was the last Chief Mechanical Engineer (CME) of the London & North Eastern Railway. He was born in Leominster in 1889 and educated at Hereford Cathedral School. In 1905 he started his career as an apprentice with the Great Northern Railway (GNR) at Doncaster. Gresley's sudden death in 1941 was a shock to all in the LNER, and although Peppercorn was considered for the role the railway's more senior man Thompson was chosen to succeed Gresley. Peppercorn retired in 1949 and died in 1951.

60504 MONS MEG (LNER 504) Rebuilt A2/2 at Doncaster Works, November 1944. Original 'P2' class, Order No 612, Works No 1839 entered traffic in 1936. The rebuilt locomotive entered traffic in November 1944. Withdrawn by BR in January 1961 and cut up in February 1961 at Doncaster Works.

Thompson A2/2 Pacific BR No 60504 MONS MEG is seen passing Chaloners Wynn Junction near York on 11 April 1953. A Kylchap exhaust arrangement was fitted with lipped chimney, as well as small wing-type smoke lifters. The locomotive carries BR Green livery with an early crest on the tender. *Norman Preedy Collection*

Mons Meg is the nickname for a famous 15th century cannon which resides on the ramparts of Edinburgh Castle overlooking the railway line as it heads out of Waverley station towards the Forth Bridge.

It is a medieval bombard in the collection of the Royal Armouries, but on loan to Historic Scotland. It was built in 1449 on the orders of Philip the Good, Duke of Burgundy and given by him to King James II, King of Scots in 1454. The bombard was employed in sieges until the middle of the 16th century, after which it was only fired on ceremonial occasions and on one such occasion in 1680 the barrel burst, rendering Mons Meg unusable. The gun remained in Edinburgh Castle until 1754 when, along with other unused weapons in Scotland, it was taken to the Tower of London. Notable author Sir Walter Scott reportedly led a successful campaign for its return. After 75 years in England, Mons Meg made a triumphant return to the castle in 1829, escorted by cavalry and infantry from the docks at Leith.

MONS MEG

THIS GIANT MEDIEVAL SIEGE GUN WAS PRESENTED TO KING JAMES II IN 1457 AND USED IN WAR AGAINST THE ENGLISH. IT WAS KEPT IN THE CASTLE AND USED ALSO FOR FIRING SALUTES. DURING ONE FIRING IN 1558, THE MASSIVE GUNSTONE WAS FOUND ALMOST 2 MILES AWAY! IT LAST FIRED IN 1681 WHEN ITS BARREL BURST.

Mons Meg has since been restored, and is now on display within Edinburgh castle grounds. It has a barrel diameter of 20 inches making it one of the largest cannons in the world, by calibre.

60510 ROBERT THE BRUCE (LNER 3699, 510 – 1946 number). A2/1 class, Works No 1950. Built at Darlington Works, entered traffic un-named in January 1945, named April 1948. Withdrawn by BR in November 1960 and cut up at Doncaster Works February 1961.

Thompson 'A2/1' class Pacific LNER No 3699 (BR 60510) is pictured adjacent to the ash pits at Edinburgh Haymarket depot in early 1945. Note the wing type smoke deflectors and ex-North Eastern 4,200 gallon 6-wheel tender. The locomotive was then un-named and seen before the completion of electric lighting installation. *Mike Morant Collection*

Robert The Bruce

Robert I (11 July 1274–7 June 1329), popularly known as Robert the Bruce, was King of Scots from 1306 until his death in 1329. Robert led Scotland during the First War of Scottish Independence against England.

He fought successfully during his reign to regain Scotland's place as an independent country and is today revered in Scotland as a national hero. Although Robert the Bruce's date of birth is known, his place of birth is less certain, although it is considered likely to have been Turnberry Castle in Ayrshire, the head of his mother's earldom. Bruce was crowned King of Scots at Scone, near Perth, on Palm Sunday.

His most famous victory undoubtedly took place at the Battle of Bannockburn, in 1314. Edward II of England reportedly assembled the largest ever army to invade Scotland. The defenders whilst being outnumbered by at least two to one nevertheless handed a crushing defeat to the English.

In 1932 the Bannockburn Preservation Committee, under Edward Bruce, 10th Earl of Elgin and Kincardine, presented lands to the National Trust for Scotland. Further lands were purchased in 1960 and 1965 to facilitate visitor access. A modern monument was erected in a field above the possible site of the battle, where the warring parties are believed to have camped on the night before the battle. *Len Mills*

Thompson 'A2/1' class Pacific BR No 60510 ROBERT THE BRUCE passes Craigentinny as it passes through the Edinburgh suburbs on the way to Waverley station, circa 1955. The Pacific had been fitted with smoke deflectors and named in 1948. Note that in 1949 it is was coupled with an 8-wheel LNER tender. The locomotive carried BR Green livery. *Norman Preedy Collection*

Statue of Robert the Bruce in the grounds of Stirling Castle. *Len Mills*

Statue of Robert the Bruce King of Scots incorporated into the Bannockburn Visitor Centre. The centre is administered by National Trust Scotland. Visit *battleofbannockburn.com/visit/*. *Len Mills*

Gresley LNER 'V2' class 2-6-2

'V2' construction at Darlington Works, July 1937. *Keith Langston Collection*

This Mixed Traffic (6MT) class of 2-6-2 (Prairie) 3-cylinder locomotives was introduced between 1936 and 1944 (throughout the WWII years). There were 184 of the class built, 160 at Darlington Works and 24 at Doncaster Works (BR 60800–60983). For a period one locomotive was fitted with a stovepipe chimney and 8 were fitted with double chimneys in 1960/61.

The first locomotive into traffic was LNER No 4771 (BR 60800) named GREEN ARROW in 1936 to coincide with the introduction of a fast freight service of the same name, that locomotive is preserved. This was the first class of 3-cylinder 2-6-2 engines to appear in Britain. They were a successful design and often proved capable of putting in performances similar to the LNER

The larger than normal nameplate of 'V2' class BR No 60809, note the regimental crest. *Ian Turnbull/Rail Photoprints*

Pacifics when rostered to top link duties. They were often referred to as 'the engines that helped to win the war' as they were an important element in keeping traffic moving on the East Coast route, often under difficult wartime conditions. The 'V2' locomotives were allocated to all parts of the LNER although most were posted to depots serving the ECML between London and Aberdeen. There were 8 locomotives of the class named and of those, 5 had direct military links. The often larger than normal nameplates of a distinctive design were mounted over the central driving wheel splasher.

60809 THE SNAPPER (LNER 4780, 709 and 809 – 1946 number) built at Darlington Works. Entered traffic in September 1937. Withdrawn by BR in July 1964 and cut up in October 1964 at Swindon Works (allocated to Darlington for scrapping but transferred to Swindon).

Gresley 'V2' class BR No 60809 THE SNAPPER THE EAST YORKSHIRE REGIMENT, THE DUKE OF YORK'S OWN is seen with LNER Green lined livery when between turns at its then home shed Heaton, Newcastle, circa1958. The large distinctive regimental nameplate with crest can be clearly seen. *Norman Preedy Collection*

The East Yorkshire Regiment was a line infantry regiment of the British Army, which was first raised in 1685 as Sir William Clifton's Regiment of Foot, renamed the 15th Regiment of Foot. In 1935, the regiment was renamed The East Yorkshire Regiment (The Duke of York's Own), after its Colonel-in-Chief.

Later the regiment amalgamated with the Green Howards and the Duke of Wellington's Regiment (West Riding) to form the Yorkshire Regiment.

The **SNAPPER** nickname owes its origin to an incident at the Battle of Brandywine (American War of Independence). After running short of ammunition some of the troops were ordered to 'snap their flints' firing only small powder charges, whilst the best marksmen were allocated the dwindling supply of shot. The bluff worked and the '15th' won the battle.

Troops from the East Yorkshire Regiment take cover behind a bank as an enemy shell explodes nearby, 19 July 1944. *Sgt. Christie No 5 Army Film and Photographic Unit*

60835 THE GREEN HOWARD ALEXANDRA, PRINCESS OF WALES'S OWN YORKSHIRE REGIMENT (LNER 4806, 735 and 835 – 1946 number) built at Darlington Works. Entered traffic in September 1938. Withdrawn by BR in October 1965 and cut up in February 1966 by GH Campbell, Airdrie.

LMS 'Royal Scot' class 4-6-0 BR No 46133 carried the name THE GREEN HOWARDS.

Gresley 'V2' class BR No 60835 THE GREEN HOWARD ALEXANDRA, PRINCESS OF WALES'S OWN YORKSHIRE REGIMENT in BR Black livery seen at Glasgow Buchanan Street station after arriving with the 13.30 service from Aberdeen, on 28 March 1964. Note the trucks loaded with mail bags on the platform. Note that the locomotive nameplate used the singular 'HOWARD' whilst the official regimental name uses the plural 'HOWARDS'. *Ian Turnbull/Rail Photoprints*

Green Howards (Alexandra, Princess of Wales's Own Yorkshire Regiment).

The regiment was first raised in Devon in November 1688 and a second regiment was raised some four months later. The two subsequently coming under the same commander, were known as the 1st and 2nd Battalions of the 19th Regiment of Foot. In 1744 it was general practice to name a regiment after its Colonel, then the Honourable Charles Howard, thus the first became known as the 'Green Howards'. This was to distinguish it from another regiment serving in that time period, but commanded by a different Colonel Howard. Consequently, the colour of the regiments' uniform facings was used as the distinguishing feature, thus creating the names Green Howards and the Buff Howards. The regiment was first affiliated to the North Riding of Yorkshire in 1782 being titled the 19th (First Yorkshire North Riding Regiment) of Foot, Richmond became the regiment's base in 1873. In 1920 the title became The Green Howards (Alexandra, Princess of Wales's Own Yorkshire Regiment). In 2006 it became part of the Yorkshire Regiment.

Regimental cap badge.

Gresley 'V2' class BR No 60835 THE GREEN HOWARD ALEXANDRA, PRINCESS OF WALES'S OWN YORKSHIRE REGIMENT is seen on shed at Darlington in November 1958. Note the regimental crest on the nameplate and the later style BR tender logo. *BKB Green/Norman Preedy Collection*

Gresley 'V2' class BR No 60835 THE GREEN HOWARD ALEXANDRA, PRINCESS OF WALES'S OWN YORKSHIRE REGIMENT is seen at Haymarket depot after a visit to the coaling plant in 1957. Note the early style BR tender logo. *David Anderson*

60872 KING'S OWN YORKSHIRE LIGHT INFANTRY (LNER 4843, 772 and 872 – 1946 number) built at Doncaster Works, Works No 1898. Entered traffic in April 1939. Withdrawn by BR in September 1963 and cut up in October 1963 at Doncaster Works.

Gresley 'V2' class BR No 60872 KING'S OWN YORKSHIRE LIGHT INFANTRY passes High Dyke with the 09.14 York–Kings Cross service, on 19 August 1961.
Hugh Ballantyne/Rail Photoprints

The King's Own Yorkshire Light Infantry (KOYLI) was a light infantry regiment of the British Army. It officially existed from 1881 to 1968, but its predecessors go back to 1755.

The 53rd Regiment of Foot was raised in Leeds in 1755 and renumbered the 51st in January 1757. In 1782, in common with other regiments of the line, the 51st was given a county designation, becoming the 51st (2nd Yorkshire, West Riding) Regiment of Foot. The title of Light Infantry was given in honour of its former commander General Sir John Moore in 1809, and in 1821 the regiment was given royal status when King's Own was added to its title, becoming the 51st (2nd Yorkshire, West Riding, The King's Own Light Infantry) Regiment. In 1968, the regiment was amalgamated with others to become The Light Infantry, which in turn was merged with the Devonshire and Dorset Regiment, the Royal Gloucestershire, Berkshire and Wiltshire Regiment and the Royal Green Jackets to become The Rifles in 2007.

A fighting patrol of the 1/4th Battalion, KOYLI in North West Europe on 2 March 1945.
Sgt Laing No 5 Army Film and Photographic Unit

Gresley 'V2' class BR No 60872 KING'S OWN YORKSHIRE LIGHT INFANTRY seen at Doncaster depot on 25 September 1955, note the regimental crest on the nameplate. The locomotive is in the company of 'WD' Austerity 2-8-0 BR No 90538. *BKB Green/Norman Preedy Collection*

Gresley 'V2' class BR No 60872 KING'S OWN YORKSHIRE LIGHT INFANTRY is again seen at Doncaster, depot but on this occasion in the winter of 1962. *Rail Photoprints Collection*

60873 COLDSTREAMER (LNER 4844, 773 and 873 – 1946 number) built at Doncaster Works, Works No 1899. Entered traffic in May 1939. Withdrawn by BR in December 1962 and cut up in September 1963 at Cowlairs Works.

LMS 'Royal Scot' class 4-6-0 BR No 46114 was named Coldstream Guardsman.

Gresley 'V2' class BR No 60873 COLDSTREAMER is seen at Haymarket depot in September 1958. Note that the nameplate is complemented by a regimental crest. *David Anderson*

The Coldstream Guards is a part of the Guards Division, Foot Guards regiments of the British Army.

It is the oldest regiment in the Regular Army in continuous active service, originating in the town and parish of Coldstream, Scotland. The regiment was founded by General George Monck. On 13 August 1650 Monck took men from the regiments of George Fenwick and Sir Arthur Haselrig, five companies each, and formed Monck's Regiment of Foot. The origin of the regiment lies in the English Civil War when Oliver Cromwell gave Colonel George Monck permission to form his own regiment as part of the New Model Army. It is one of two regiments of the Household Division

that can trace its lineage to the New Model Army, the other being the Blues and Royals (Royal Horse Guards and 1st Dragoons).

60964 THE DURHAM LIGHT INFANTRY (LNER 3676, 864 and 964 – 1946 number) built at Darlington Works, Works No 1904. Entered traffic un-named in January 1943. Named in a ceremony at Durham on 29 April 1958. Withdrawn by BR in May 1964 and cut up in October 1964 at Swindon Works.

The nameplate of Gresley 'V2' class BR No 60964, note the regimental crest. The locomotive was named on Platform 5 at Durham station on 29 April 1958. *Ian Talbot/Rail Photoprints*

The Durham Light Infantry was a light infantry regiment of the British Army in existence from 1881 to 1968. It was formed in 1881 under the Childers Reforms by the amalgamation of the 68th (Durham) Regiment of Foot (Light Infantry) and the 106th Regiment of Foot (Bombay Light Infantry) along with the Militia and Volunteers of County Durham. A new regimental badge was to be worn, depicting a Tudor rose, this was never worn on any article of clothing, but did appear on the colours until 1934. Instead the light infantry bugle horn was modified with a crown and the regiment's abbreviation DLI. In 1968 it was announced that the Durham Light Infantry would join with three other county light infantry regiments to form one large Regiment, The Light Infantry, it was to be renamed the 4th battalion the Light Infantry. On 12 December 1968 the 1st battalion laid up its colours in a service in Durham Cathedral, attended by Princess Alexandra, the Regiment's last Colonel in Chief.

A signals section of the 13th Battalion, Durham Light Infantry, equipped with telescopes, field telephone and signalling lamps, await news of the progress of the unit's attack towards Veldhoek during the Battle of Menin Road. *John Warwick Brooke*

Gresley 'V2' class BR No 60964 THE DURHAM LIGHT INFANTRY is seen on Platform No 5 at Durham station during the locomotive's naming ceremony on 29 April 1958. *David Anderson Collection*

The date of the ceremony was chosen to celebrate the bicentenary of the raising of The Durham Light Infantry Regiment. The naming of the locomotive by British Railways (BR) came about after a fortuitous meeting between Col. G.K. Stobart formally of the regiment and Mr T.H. Summerson, Chairman of the North Eastern Region BR. The gentlemen were taking part in a grouse shoot when the colonel seized an opportunity to engage Mr Summerson in conversation, and succeeded in persuading him to name a locomotive for the regiment.

The locomotive chosen was the Darlington Works built Gresley 'V2' class 2-6-2 BR No 60964. The nameplate with regimental badge was cast in the pattern shop at Doncaster Works. During what the regimental journal later recorded as being a fine afternoon, the buglers of the 1st Battalion sounded a fanfare as the official party arrived on the station platform. The party included Mr Summerson accompanied by the Mayor and Mayoress of Durham together with Col. Mark Leather who was invited to christen the engine. Col. Leather unveiled the nameplate and also presented tokens to Driver Blacklock and Fireman Gordon. Both these men had served in the regiment, Blacklock in the 5th Battalion during the First World War and Gordon who completed his National Service with the regiment, 1953/54. After the conclusion of the ceremony several children were allowed on the locomotive footplate for rides up and down the platform. British Railways provided the assembled company with tea served in the station buffet.

The Durham Light Infantry memorial, National Memorial Arboretum. *Harry Mitchell*

Gresley 'V2' class BR No 60964 THE DURHAM LIGHT INFANTRY is seen passing Dringhouses, York with an express service in 1959. *Norman Preedy Collection*

The driver of Gresley 'V2' class BR No 60964 THE DURHAM LIGHT INFANTRY eases his locomotive forward after servicing and before its next turn of duty, York circa 1960. *Mike Stokes Collection*

GCR Robinson B8 class 4-6-0 'Glenalmond'

This class of 2-cylinder 4-6-0 locomotives was introduced between 1913 and 1915. When introduced they were given a power rating of 5MT. The 'B8' was a smaller-wheeled version of Robinson's B2 Sir Sam Fay class, and were known as the 'Glen Almonds' after the prototype locomotive Glenalmond.

There were originally 11 members of the class and their construction took place at Gorton Works. The 'B8' class were mainly used on goods trains and slow passenger/excursion services. During the Second World War, the B8s were used on a variety of traffic including heavy goods services and troop trains. Five locomotives of this mixed traffic class came into BR stock but were scrapped without receiving their allocated BR numbers which were Nos 61353–61355 and 61357–61358 (those numbers were reallocated to new 'B1' class locomotives). Two of the 'B8' class engines were given names with military connections.

LNER No 5442 an unnamed example of the class, is seen on shed at Annersley in July 1937. *Norman Preedy Collection*

5446 EARL ROBERTS OF KANDAHAR (GCR 446, LNER 1357 – 1946 number) built at Gorton Works. Entered traffic in November 1914. BR No 61357* allocated but never carried. Withdrawn by BR in April 1949 and cut up at Dukinfield Carriage Works.

BR Standard Britannia Pacific No 70042 carried the name LORD ROBERTS

Garter encircled shield of arms of Frederick Sleigh Roberts, 1st Earl Roberts.

Field Marshal Frederick Sleigh Roberts, 1st Earl Roberts, VC, KG, KP, GCB, OM, GCSI, GCIE, KStJ, VD, PC, FRSGS. He was born 30 September 1832, in Kanpur, India and died 14 November 1914, in Saint-Omer, France. Roberts was educated at Eton, Sandhurst, and Addiscombe Military Seminary before entering the East India Company Army as a second lieutenant with the Bengal Artillery on 12 December 1851. He became Aide-de-Camp to his father, General Sir Abraham Roberts in 1852, transferred to the Bengal Horse Artillery in 1854 and was promoted to lieutenant on 31 May 1857. He subsequently became one of the most successful British military commanders of his time. He served in the Indian Rebellion, the Expedition to Abyssinia and the Second Anglo-Afghan War before leading British Forces to success in the Second Boer War. He also became the last Commander-in-Chief of the Forces before the post was abolished in 1904.

5279 EARL KITCHENER OF KHARTOUM (GCR 279, LNER 1358 – 1946 number) built at Gorton Works. Entered traffic in December 1914. BR No 61358 allocated but never carried. Withdrawn by BR in August 1948 and cut up at Dukinfield Carriage Works.

BR Standard Britannia Pacific No 70043 carried the name LORD KITCHENER

EARL KITCHENER OF KHARTOUM. Field Marshal Horatio Herbert Kitchener, 1st Earl Kitchener, KG, KP, GCB, OM, GCSI, GCMG, GCIE, PC.

He was a senior British Army officer and colonial administrator who won notoriety for his imperial campaigns against the Boers during the Second Boer War. Kitchener was credited in 1898 for winning the Battle of Omdurman and securing control of the Sudan for which he was made Lord Kitchener of Khartoum, becoming a qualifying peer and of mid-rank as an Earl. As Chief of Staff (1900–1902) in the Second Boer War he played a key role in Lord Roberts' conquest of the Boer Republics. In 1914, Kitchener became Secretary of State for War, a Cabinet Minister. One of the few to foresee a long war, lasting for at least three years, and with the authority to act effectively on that perception, he organised the largest volunteer army that Britain had seen, and oversaw a significant expansion of materials production to fight on the Western Front. On 5 June 1916, Kitchener was making his way to Russia to attend negotiations, on HMS *Hampshire*, when it struck a German mine 1.5 miles west of the Orkneys, Scotland, and sank. Kitchener was among the 737 persons who perished.

Famous recruiting poster featuring Field Marshal Kitchener.

Gresley LNER 'B17' class 4-6-0 'Sandringham'

This class of 3-cylinder 4-6-0 locomotives was introduced between 1928 and 1937, BR Nos 61600 – 61672. When introduced they were given a power rating of 4P but were reclassified by British Railways to 5P in 1953. There were 73 members of the class and their construction took place at Darlington Works (52) and also by the contractors North British Locomotive Co (10) and Robert Stephenson & Co Ltd (11). They were further categorised as 'B17/1' the first 48 engines originally coupled with Great Eastern Railway (GER) type tenders, 'B17/2' and 'B17/3' which were variants of 'B17/1' but were included in that sub class prior to 1948.

The last 25 engines of the class were designated 'B17/4' and were coupled with larger LNER type tenders.

Two locomotives were rebuilt as streamlined engines (similar to the Gresley 'A4' class) and they were designated 'B17/5'. When most of the class were later rebuilt with larger boilers (1943 onwards) they were designated 'B17/6'. From 1945 onwards Thompson rebuilt ten of the class with 'B1' type boilers. All of the class were named, 48 locomotives after country houses (hence Sandringham), 25 after football clubs.

There were three 'B17/6' locomotives with military connected names, the names were carried over the central driving wheel splasher.

61605 LINCOLNSHIRE REGIMENT (LNER 2805, 1605 – 1946 number) built by North British Locomotive Co. Ltd, Works No 23808. Entered traffic in December 1928 as BURNHAM THORPE. Renamed in April 1938. Rebuilt as 'B17/6' in January 1948, BR No 61605. Withdrawn by BR in May 1958 and cut up in July 1958 at Doncaster Works.

Gresley LNER 'B17/1' class 4-6-0 'Sandringham' LNER No 2805 BURNHAM THORPE is seen with 'The Flushing Continental' somewhere on the Great Eastern Railway (GER) mainline to Shenfield. The image is dated between 1932 and 1938. The locomotive was renamed LINCOLNSHIRE REGIMENT in 1938. Note, Flushing is the English bastardisation of the Dutch place name 'Vlissingen'. *Mike Morant Collection*

The Royal Lincolnshire Regiment was a line infantry regiment of the British Army raised on 20 June 1685 as the Earl of Bath's Regiment for its first Colonel, John Granville, 1st Earl of Bath. In 1751, it was numbered and named the 10th (North Lincoln) Regiment of Foot. After the Childers Reforms of 1881, it became the Lincolnshire Regiment after the county where it had been recruiting since 1781.

After the Second World War, the regiment was honoured with the name Royal Lincolnshire Regiment, before being amalgamated in 1960 with the Northamptonshire Regiment to form the 2nd East Anglian Regiment (Duchess of Gloucester's Own Royal Lincolnshire and Northamptonshire).

The John Granville, 1st Earl of Bath (1628–1701), 1860 stained glass window in Granville Chapel, Church of St James the Great, Kilkhampton, Cornwall.

61645 THE SUFFOLK REGIMENT (LNER 2845, 1645 -1946 number) built at Darlington Works. Entered traffic in June 1935. Named in a ceremony at Bury St. Edmunds station on 27 June 1935. Rebuilt as 'B17/6' in December 1952. Withdrawn by BR in February 1959 and cut up in April 1959 at Doncaster Works.

Gresley LNER 'B17/6' class 4-6-0 'Sandringham' BR No 61645 THE SUFFOLK REGIMENT is seen on a turntable at the depot thought to be Stratford in 1952, the name plate is complemented by a regimental crest mounted on the wheel splasher and the Darlington Works plate is located on the forward driving wheel splasher. Note that the tender had not at that time received a BR logo. *Rail Photoprints Collection*

The Suffolk Regiment was an infantry regiment of the line in the British Army with a history dating back to 1685. The regiment was raised by Henry Howard, 7th Duke of Norfolk as the Duke of Norfolk's Regiment of Foot in 1685 and included men from the East Anglian counties of Norfolk and Suffolk. It was originally formed to combat the Monmouth Rebellion, but was not disbanded when the rebellion was defeated. It saw service for three centuries before being amalgamated with the Royal Norfolk Regiment to form the 1st East Anglian Regiment (Royal Norfolk and Suffolk) in 1959.

HM King George VI is seen with men of the Suffolk Regiment during a tour of Western Command, on 23 October 1941.
Lt. Taylor War Photographer

61658 THE ESSEX REGIMENT (LNER 2858, 1658 – 1946 number) built at Darlington Works. Entered traffic in May 1936 as NEWCASTLE UNITED. Renamed in June 1936. Rebuilt as 'B17/6' in September 1950. Withdrawn by BR in December 1959 and cut up in February 1960 at Doncaster Works.

Gresley LNER 'B17/6' class 4-6-0 'Sandringham' BR No 61658 THE ESSEX REGIMENT is seen at Retford Crossing with a boat train for Hull, during Coronation week June 1953. *David Anderson Collection*

The Essex Regiment was a line infantry regiment of the British Army which was in existence from 1881 to 1958. It was formed in 1881 under the Childers Reforms by the amalgamation of the 44th (East Essex) Regiment of Foot and the 56th (West Essex) Regiment of Foot. In 1958, the Essex Regiment was amalgamated with the Bedfordshire and Hertfordshire Regiment to form the 3rd East Anglian Regiment (16th/44th Foot). However, in 1964 it was amalgamated again, this time with the 1st East Anglian Regiment (Royal Norfolk and Suffolk), the 2nd East Anglian Regiment (Duchess of Gloucester's Own Royal Lincolnshire and Northamptonshire) and the Royal Leicestershire Regiment to form the Royal Anglian Regiment. The lineage of the Essex Regiment is continued by 'C' Company of the 1st Battalion of the Royal Anglian Regiment.

A battery of 3-inch mortars of the Essex Regiment is seen in action, December 1942. *Lt. Cook, War Office Official Photographer*

'Men of Essex. Your King and Country Need You'. Recruitment poster for Kitchener's Army, circa 1915.

GNoSR Pickersgill 'D40' class 4-4-0

Preserved ex Great North of Scotland Railway 'D40' class No 49 GORDON HIGHLANDER (BR No 62277) is seen at Auchterless, on the line from MacDuff to Inverurie on the second day of the SLS/RCTS Joint Scottish Tour, 13 June 1960. *C.J. Gammell/Mike Morant Collection*

Between 1899 and 1921 the Great North of Scotland Railway (GNoSR) introduced a William Pickersgill designed class of 2-cylinder 4-4-0 locomotive which were designated 'V' class (BR number series 62260–62262, 62264–62265, 62267–62273) and rated at 2P which was reclassified 1P by BR in 1953. In addition to the North British Locomotive Co. (NBL), other 'D40' class variants were built by Neilson, Reid & Co Ltd and also at Inverurie Works. In 1920/21 Thomas Heywood introduced a superheated version of the class with piston valves and extended smoke boxes (BR number series 62274–62279) those locomotives were designated GNoSR 'F' class, and the 4-4-0 engines were the first of that railway's fleet to be officially given names. BR took into stock 18 locomotives of this class. The NBL batch of 5 with BR numbers 62275–62279 (GNoSR Nos 47 – 50, 52), were built at Hyde Park Works as part of an GNoSR 'F' class batch of 6 locomotives to order number L730, one of that batch LNER No 2280 (GNoSR No 54) was scrapped prior to 1948. This class is perhaps better known by the LNER designation of 'D40' class.

62277 GORDON HIGHLANDER (GNoSR 49, LNER 2277) built by North British Locomotive Co. Entered traffic in October 1920. Withdrawn by BR in June 1958 and saved for preservation. **P**

LMS 'Royal Scot' class 4-6-0 BR No 46106 was also named GORDON HIGHLANDER.

The Gordon Highlanders was a line infantry regiment of the British Army that existed for 113 years, from 1881 until 1994, when it was amalgamated with the Queen's Own Highlanders (Seaforth and Camerons) to form the Highlanders (Seaforth, Gordons and Camerons). The regiment was formed on 1 July 1881 instigated under the Childers Reforms. The new two-battalion regiment was formed out of the 75th (Stirlingshire) Regiment of Foot, which became the 1st Battalion of the new regiment, and the 92nd (Gordon Highlanders) Regiment of Foot, which became the 2nd Battalion.

Gordon Highlanders cap badge.

LNER 'D40' class BR No 62277 GORDON HIGHLANDER is seen with a two-coach local train at Craigellachie station in 1953, in this delightful east facing view. The station was opened as Strathspey Junction in July 1863 and closed by BR in May 1968. It was situated on the Boat of Garten to Dufftown route (Strathspey Railway). *Norman Preedy Collection*

The locomotive spent its working life up to withdrawal in GNoSR territory. During its life under BR ownership it was initially based at Kittybrewster. It was reallocated to Keith depot in June 1951, from where it was withdrawn in June 1958 as the last working member of the class. It was then restored at Inverurie Works and was painted in the pre-Heywood green GNoSR livery (which it never carried in service) it was also renumbered as GNoSR No49. After restoration the 4-4-0 was based at Glasgow Dawsholm depot and worked on various special mainline excursion trains. In June 1966 it was placed on static display in the Glasgow Transport Museum. The locomotive was loaned to The Museum of Scottish Railways at the preserved Bo'ness & Kinneil Railway, and was reportedly based at that location in 2019.

Preserved GNoSR Pickersgill designed 'D40' class 4-4-0 GNoSR No 49 GORDON HIGHLANDER is seen leaving Dumfries for Glasgow with an 'SLS' special in June 1959. *David Anderson*

GCR Robinson 4-4-0 3P 'D11' Large Director class

Between 1920 and 1924 the GCR introduced a class of 35 Robinson-designed 2-cylinder (inside) express passenger engines all of which were named, and several of the names had military connections. Often described as one of the most handsome British designs, the locomotives were built at Gorton Works (11), Kitson & Company (12) and Armstrong Whitworth & Co (12). They were originally the GCR '11F' class which later became the LNER 'D11' class. The locomotives were known as Improved or Large Director class and were a slightly heavier development of the GCR Director '11E' class introduced in 1913, LNER 'D10' class. The Large Directors were built with deeper frames, side window cabs and a higher pitched boiler. The engines were originally built with straight framing and coupling rod splashers, which were later removed to allow better access during servicing and maintenance. There were two Large Director variants 'D11/1', which were built for the GCR and introduced between 1920–1922, 11 engines BR Nos 62660–62670 and the military linked names were all within that batch. Those names were carried on horizontal nameplates mounted centrally on the top edge of the splashers. The 24 built in 1924 were known as 'D11/2' variants and were intended mainly for use on routes with the Scottish gauge, accordingly they had cut down boiler mountings. The 'D11/2' engines were named for characters in Walter Scott novels and those names were painted onto the splashers.

62660 BUTLER-HENDERSON (GCR 506, LNER 5506–2660 – 1946 number) built at Gorton Works. Entered traffic in December 1919. Withdrawn by BR in November 1960, and saved for preservation. **P**

Capt. The Hon. Eric Brand Butler-Henderson (26 September 1884 – 18 December 1953) was the seventh child of Alexander Henderson, 1st Baron Faringdon. He was a soldier and company director.

In May 1918, Butler-Henderson was elected a Director of the Great Central Railway (GCR), where his father, Lord Faringdon, was chairman of the board. Like other GCR Directors of the period, he was accorded the honour of having one of the railway's latest express passenger locomotives named after him.

He was appointed to the Berkshire Imperial Yeomanry as a second lieutenant on 30 March 1908 and transferred to the Berkshire (Hungerford) Yeomanry on 1 April 1908, retaining his rank. He was promoted to the rank of Captain on 20 December 1915, transferring from the Yeomanry to the Territorial Force Reserve on 6 November 1917. He relinquished his Territorial Army Reserve commission on 30 September 1921, retaining his rank of Captain but not the right to wear the uniform.

LNER 'D11/1' class BR No 62660 BUTLER-HENDERSON is seen with a rake of Stanier stock at Derby Midland station, circa 1955. *Mike Morant Collection*

BUTLER-HENDERSON works plate.

The locomotive was allocated to Sheffield Darnall motive power depot at the time of its withdrawal by British Railways in October 1960. For its three operators, Great Central Railway, London North Eastern Railway and British Railways the 'D11/1' reportedly clocked up 1,280,897 miles in service. By modern standards that is really cost-efficient, when the 1919 build cost of £7,620 is taken into consideration. It was decided that the locomotive should be preserved and initially it was moved to the British Transport Commision (BTC) museum at Clapham, London and put on static display. In 1975 the BTC ceased to exist and the Robinson 4-4-0 became part of the National Collection and it was loaned to the Great Central Railway (GCR).

It was at the GCR that restoration to working order commenced in 1981 with the engine steaming again in March 1982. After a succesful period in steam and after its boiler certificate expired in 1992, the popular locomotive was moved to the National Railway Museum, York (NRM). In 2019 the locomotive was located at Barrow Hill Round House & Railway Centre, having moved there on loan from the NRM.

62665 MONS (GCR 501, LNER 5501–2665 – 1946 number) built at Gorton Works. Entered traffic in September 1922. Withdrawn by BR in May 1959 and cut up in July 1959 at Gorton Works.

'J36' class BR No 65224 also carried this name.

The Battle of **Mons** (23 August 1914) was the first major action of the British Expeditionary Force (BEF) in the First World War. It was a subsidiary action of the Battle of the Frontiers, in which the Allies clashed with Germany on the French borders. At Mons, the British Army attempted to hold the line of the Mons–Condé Canal against the German 1st Army.

The British fought well and inflicted disproportionate casualties on the numerically superior Germans, they were eventually forced to retreat due both to the greater strength of the Germans and the sudden retreat of the French Fifth Army. Though initially planned as a simple tactical withdrawal and executed in good order, the British retreat from Mons lasted for two weeks and took the BEF to the outskirts of Paris before it counter-attacked in concert with the French, at the Battle of the Marne.

A commemorative plaque dedicated to the regiment of the BEF who fought at Mons in August 1914. *Jean-Pol Grandmont*

62666 ZEEBRUGGE (GCR 502, LNER 5502–2666 – 1946 number) built at Gorton Works. Entered traffic in October 1922. Withdrawn by BR in December 1960 and cut up in December 1960 at Doncaster Works.

Ex GC 'Director' D11/1 BR No 62666 ZEEBRUGGE passes Bourne End with a 'Northern Rubber Special' working from Retford to Windsor & Eton, on 7 June 1953. *Dave Cobbe Collection/Rail Photoprints*

Zeebrugge Raid on 23 April 1918 was an attempt by the Royal Navy to block the Belgian port of Bruges-Zeebrugge. The British intended to sink obsolete ships in the canal entrance, to prevent German vessels from leaving port. The port was used by the Imperial German Navy as a base for U-boats and light shipping. Several attempts to close the Flanders ports by naval bombardment failed and Operation Hush, a 1917 plan to advance up the coast, also proved abortive. As U-boats attacks increased, finding a way to close the ports became even more urgent. An attempt to raid Zeebrugge was made on 2 April 1918 but was cancelled at the last moment, after the wind direction changed and made it impossible to lay a smokescreen to cover the ships.

A second attempt was made on 23 April, taking place at the same time as an attack on Ostend. Blockships were scuttled obstructing the narrowest part of the Bruges Canal and one of two submarines rammed the viaduct linking the shore and the mole.

The blockships were evidently sunk in the wrong place and subsequently the Germans reopened the canal to submarines, during high tides.

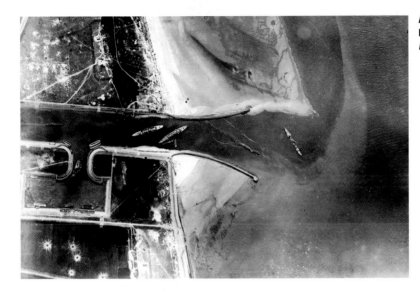

Aerial photograph showing aftermath of the Zeebrugge Raid. British blockships are, left–right: *HMS Intrepid*, *HMS Iphigenia* and *HMS Thetis*.

Ex GC 'Director' D11/1 BR No 62666 ZEEBRUGGE is seen at Doncaster station with the 1.12pm Doncaster to Barnsley local service, on 9 September 1953. Note the large number of presumably, school lunch-time admirers. *BKB Green/Norman Preedy Archive*

62667 SOMME (GCR 503, LNER 5503–2667 – 1946 number) built at Gorton Works. Entered traffic in November 1922. Withdrawn by BR in August 1960 and cut up in September 1960 at Doncaster Works.

'J36' class BR No 65222 also carried this name.

Ex GC 'Director' D11/1 BR No 62667 SOMME is seen at Shireoaks, with the RCTS 'South Yorkshire Railtour No 2' on 7 June 1953. The 'D11/1' was in charge of the train from Sheffield Midland to Elsecar on the outward journey, with 'J11' class BR No 64374 taking charge between Elsecar & City and Elsecar Junction. Electric locomotive No E26013 took the train from Elsecar Junction via Penistone to Wombwell Exchange Sidings. The 'D11/1' then headed the return journey to Sheffield Midland from Wombwell E.S. *RCTS Archive*

Somme. The combined forces of the British Empire and French Third Republic fought the Battle of the Somme against the German Empire during World War I. It took place along a 15-mile front between 1 July and 18 November 1916, on both sides of the upper reaches of the River Somme in France. The battle was intended to hasten a victory for the Allies and was the largest battle of the First World War on the Western Front. The Battle of the Somme has the distinction of being the first battle in which tanks were used. During the first day of battle a staggering 19,240 British soldiers were killed, making that day the bloodiest in the history of the British Army. The Battle of the Somme is generally thought of as a ground offensive but there were in addition aerial elements. The Royal Flying Corps (the forerunner to the RAF) lost 800 aircraft and 252 aircrew were killed. More than three million men fought in the battle and one million men were wounded or killed. The casualties reportedly totalled 1,123,907, comprising of 419,654 British, 204,253 French and 500,000 German.

An early model British Mark I 'male' tank, named C-15, near Thiepval, 25 September 1916. Note that the tank is fitted with the wire 'grenade shield' and steering tail, both features which were discarded in the next models.

RFC recruiting poster.

Ex GC 'Director' D11/1 BR No 62667 SOMME is seen at Trafford Park depot on 23 August 1952, note also sister engine BR No 62666. Note the dilapidated roof of the engine shed which was one of the last to have a steam locomotive allocation. *BKB Green/Norman Preedy Archive*

Trafford Park depot was originally part of the Cheshire Lines Railway which under BR had the shed codes 19F (1948–1949), 13A (1949), 9E (1949–1956), 17F (1957–1958) and 9E (1958–1968). During the 1950's the depot was home to a number of ex-Great Central Railway Robinson 'D10' and 'D11/1' locomotives which worked out their last years on fast and semi-fast passenger services over the ex-Cheshire Lines Committee routes. They were often to be seen on services between Manchester and Liverpool via Warrington Central, and Manchester and Chester via Northwich.

Ex GC 'Director' D11/1 BR No 62667 SOMME is seen at Elsecar which is located on the southern part of the former South Yorkshire Railway freight-only branch, which ran from Elsecar Junction on the former Mexborough to Barnsley Line. The 'D11/1' has just arrived with the RCTS 'South Yorkshire Railtour No 2' on 7 June 1953. *RCTS Archive*

LMS 'Jubilee' class BR No 45684 also carried this name.

Ex GC 'Director' D11/1 BR No 62668 JUTLAND is seen at Retford with a Sheffield-Cleethorpes service in August 1958. *J Davenport/Norman Preedy Archive*

Jutland. The Battle of Jutland was a naval battle fought between Britain's Royal Navy Grand Fleet, under Admiral Sir John Jellicoe, and the Imperial German Navy's High Seas Fleet, under Vice-Admiral Reinhard Scheer, during the First World War. The battle involved extensive manoeuvring and was categorised as effectively consisting of three main engagements, namely the battlecruiser action, the fleet action and the night action, which took part over the period 31 May to 1 June 1916, in the North Sea of the coast of the Jutland Peninsula, Denmark. For the British, 151 combat ships of which 28 were battleships, fought against 99 German vessels of which 16 were battleships. It was the largest naval battle and the only full-scale clash of battleships in the Great War. Notably the Battle of Jutland was the third fleet action between steel battleships. Jutland was the last major battle in world history fought primarily by battleships. Both sides claimed victory and casualties on both sides were high, 6,094 killed and 674 wounded on the British side and 2551 killed and 507 wounded on the German side. The British lost more ships and twice as many sailors but succeeded in containing the German fleet. The British press criticised the Grand Fleet's failure to force a decisive outcome, while Scheer's plan of destroying a substantial portion of the British fleet also failed. The British strategy of denying Germany access to both the United Kingdom and the Atlantic did succeed, which was the stated British long-term goal.

HMS *Caroline*, a 'C-class' light cruiser which took part in the Battle of Jutland is seen in 1917. The ship is the last survivor of the battle to still be afloat. The vessel is now used as a museum ship at Alexandra Dock in the Titanic Quarter, Belfast. *Surgeon Oscar Parkes*

62669 YPRES (GCR 505, LNER 5505–2669 – 1946 number) built at Gorton Works. Entered traffic in December 1922. Withdrawn by BR in August 1960 and cut up in that month 1960 at Doncaster Works.

'J36' class LNER No 5269 also carried this name.

Ex GC 'Director' D11/1 BR No 62669 YPRES is seen whilst carrying out a positioning move at Penistone station in 1952. *J Davenport/Norman Preedy Archive*

Ypres. The Battle of Ypres was a series of engagements during the First World War, fought near the Belgian city of Ypres in West Flanders, between the Allied armies of Belgium, France, the British and Canadian Expeditionary Forces and the German Empire. There were five engagements in which there were hundreds of thousands of casualties. The battles were:

First Battle of Ypres, (19 October–22 November 1914).
Second Battle of Ypres, (22 April–15 May 1915). The first mass use of poison gas by the German army.
Battle of Passchendaele, also known as the Third Battle of Ypres (31 July–10 November 1917).
Battle of the Lys, also known as the Battle of Estaires and the Fourth Battle of Ypres (9 April–29 April 1918).
Fifth Battle of Ypres, also known as Advance of Flanders and Battle of the Peaks of Flanders (28 September–2 October 1918).

The 'Menin Gate Memorial to the Missing'. It is located near Ypres in West Flanders, Belgium. Designed by Sir Reginald Blomfield it was unveiled on 24 July 1927. *Johan Bakker*

Ex GC 'Director' D11/1 LNER No 5505 YPRES (became BR No 62669 is seen at Neasden depot on 7 June 1937. *RCTS Archive*

Ex GC 'Director' D11/1 BR No 62669 YPRES is seen adjacent to the turntable at Northwich depot during 1955. Note the temporary cover over the rear tender wheel which had been placed there whilst an axle box repair was being carried out. *Rail Photoprints Collection*

62670 MARNE (GCR 511, LNER 5511–2670 – 1946 number) built at Gorton Works. Entered traffic in December 1922. Withdrawn by BR in November 1960 and cut up in January 1961 at Doncaster Works.

'J36' class LNER NO 9666 also carried this name.

Ex GC 'Director' D11/1 BR No 62670 is seen between turns at Trafford Park depot on 12 May 1951. *BKB Green/Norman Preedy Archive*

Marne. The first Battle of the Marne also known as the Miracle of the Marne, was a World War I battle fought from 6–12 September 1914. It resulted in an Allied victory against the German armies in the west. The battle was the culmination of the German advance into France and pursuit of the Allied armies which followed the Battle of the Frontiers in August and had reached the eastern outskirts of Paris. A counter-attack by six French armies and the British Expeditionary Force (BEF) along the Marne River forced the Imperial German Army to retreat in a northwesterly direction. The battle of the Marne was a major turning point of World War I. By the end of August 1914, the whole Allied army on the Western Front had been forced into a general retreat back towards Paris. Meanwhile, the two main German armies continued to advance through France. It seemed that Paris would be taken as both the French and

The memorial chapel to the Battles of the Marne located in Dormans, in the Grand Est region of France.

the British forces fell back towards the Marne River. However, the war became a stalemate when the Allied Powers won the Battle of the Marne. It was the first major clash on the Western Front and one of the most important events in the war.

The Second Battle of the Marne was fought from 15 July–6 August 1918 by Britain together with France, the United States and Italy. It was significantly the German Empire's last major offensive of the war on the Western Front and it resulted in an allied victory. The Germans retreated in the face of an unyielding Allied advance which some 100 or so days later culminated in the Armistice with Germany.

NBR Holmes 0-6-0 2F 'J36' class

LNER 'J36' class (ex-North British Railway 'C' class) 0-6-0 BR No 65243 which carried the name MAUDE, is seen with a mixed freight train consisting mainly of vans on 8 June 1957. The location is between Gorgie and Craiglockhart stations on the Edinburgh Suburban Line. The locomotive did not carry its name on this occasion. The later to be preserved 'J36', was in BR Black unlined freight locomotive livery and it is apparent that the recently carried out repainting did not include the addition of a name. It was unusual in British locomotive history for freight engines to carry names however, many of the named 'J36' locomotives survived into nationalisation (1948) still carrying their painted commemorative titles applied to follow the curve of the central driving wheel splasher. It was not uncommon for works repaints to omit the names but many were later restored by shed staff at their home depots. *David Anderson*

There were 168 locomotives of the Holmes designed North British Railway (NBR) 2-cylinder 'C' class built between 1888 and 1900, and at that time they were the most numerous NBR class of engines. The London & North Eastern Railway (LNER) redesignated the class as 'J36'. Of the 123 members of the class which came into British Railways stock in 1948, 101 were built at Cowlairs Works, 9 at Neilson & Co Ltd and 13 at Sharp Stewart and Co. A total of 25 engines of the class which were commandeered by the Government to serve overseas with the Railway Operating Department (ROD) during World War I, were commemorated on their return to the NBR between April and July 1919 by being given the names of well-known military leaders and major battles of the aforementioned conflict. This section details the 12 of those locomotives which came into the BR 1948 stock list.

65216 (NBR 628, LNER 9628–5216 – 1946 number) built at Cowlairs Works. Entered traffic in January 1890. Named BYNG after returning from ROD service, 1919. Withdrawn by BR in April 1962, and cut up by P.W. McLellan in April 1963.

LNER 'J36' class BR No 65216 BYNG is seen between duties at Carlisle Canal depot circa 1949, note the name painted on the centre wheel splasher and BRITISH RAILWAYS still shown on the tender. *Norman Preedy Archive*

LNER 'J36' class BR No 65216 BYNG is again seen at Carlisle Canal depot this time in June 1953. Note the NBR style 2,500-gallon tender which is fitted with coal rails. *Rail Photoprints Collection*

Byng. Field Marshal Julian Hedworth George Byng, 1st Viscount Byng of Vimy. GCB, GCMG, MVO (11 September 1862–6 June 1935) was a British army officer during World War I.

Field Marshal Julian Hedworth George Byng, 1917.

From a military family, Byng joined the 10th Hussars from Eton School in 1883 and served in South Africa, Egypt and France where he took over the 3rd Cavalry Division, and later headed the Canadian Corps achieving the capture of the Vimy Ridge from the enemy. Thereafter he was transferred for service in the 3rd Army where he remained until the Armistice. Byng became Governor General of Canada between 1921–1926 and was appointed to the rank of Field Marshal in 1932. After his vice regal tenure, he became Commissioner of Police of the Metropolis and was promoted within the peerage to become Viscount Byng of Vimy. His family home was Wrotham Park, Hertfordshire however he died whilst at Thorpe Hall Essex on 6 June 1935. Lord Byng of Vimy was buried at the 11th century parish church of St. Leonard in Beaumont-cum-Moze, Essex.

The Baron and Baroness Byng of Vimy as the vice regal couple of Canada 1922.

65217 (NBR 176, LNER 9176–5217 – 1946 number) built at Cowlairs Works. Entered traffic in April 1890. Named FRENCH after returning from ROD service, 1919. Withdrawn by BR in October 1962, and cut up at Inverurie Works in May 1963.

The name of locomotive BR No 65217 together with a Cowlairs Works LNER era makers plate can be seen in this image of the engines centre wheel splasher. *Keith Langston Collection*

French. Field Marshal John Denton Pinkstone French, 1st Earl of Ypres, KP, GCB, OM, GCVO, KCMG, ADC, PC (28 September 1852–22 May 1925), known as Sir John French from 1901 to 1916, and as The Viscount French between 1916 and 1922, was a senior British Army officer.

French transferred to the army from service life in the Royal Navy in which he served from 1866 to 1870 and joined the Suffolk Militia. He later rose to command the 19th Hussars at the age of 36. Serving as a commander of a cavalry force during the Boer War, he cleared the Cape Province of rebels in 1899 and in the following year he led the Relief of Kimberley, after which action he was knighted and promoted to major general. French was appointed as Chief of the Imperial General Staff in 1912 and was promoted to Field Marshal in 1913. During World War I he took command of the British Expeditionary Force (BEF) in France. Criticised for his over optimism regarding the outcome of the First Battle of Ypres, he cooperated with the French forces in 1915, but an incapacity for military tasks led to his replacement by Field Marshal Haig and a subsequent demotion as Lord Lieutenant of Ireland from 1918 to 1921. He died at Deal Castle, Kent on 22 May 1925. His body was taken for cremation in London and thereafter his ashes were transported by military procession to Victoria station and onward to Ripple, Kent where they were buried in the graveyard of St. Mary the Virgin Church.

Field Marshal Sir John French, Commander in Chief, in France image from 18 August 1915. *British Library*

LNER 'J36' class BR No 65217 FRENCH is seen at Kipps depot in 1959. *Norman Preedy Archive*

LNER 'J36' class BR No 65217 FRENCH is again seen at Kipps depot in 1956. Note the tender cab. *Rail Photoprints Collection*

This view of BR No 65217 French shows the addition of a tender cab to good effect. The relatively open aspect of the 'J36' cabs afforded the locomotive crews limited protection from the elements. Many of the class were attached to snow ploughs and of those were fitted with tender cabs thus giving the crews much more protection. *Norman Preedy Archive*

Early mainline locomotives were not fitted with cabs and as a consequence the footplate crews had to contend with little or no protection. North British Railway 'R' class 0-6-0 No 381 is seen on 2 July 1925, at Goosepool on the way to the Stockton & Darlington Centenary locomotive parades. *Mike Morant Collection*

The so-called spectacle plate fitted to No 381 seen in the image above offered very little protection from the weather. Author John Thomas in his book *The Springburn Story* (David & Charles 1964 and 1974) recounts the tale of a North British driver in the late 1880s who having been in charge of a mineral train in particularly foul weather complained to the management saying that 'the hail peeled the skin off my face and caused it to bleed'. In response the railway company supplied the crews with overcoats, but not at that time locomotive cabs. It can be noted in that period North British locomotive men were supplied with leather gauntlets and helmets.

65222 (NBR 646, LNER 9646–5222 – 1946 number) built at Cowlairs Works. Entered traffic in February 1891. Named SOMME after returning from ROD service, 1919. Withdrawn by BR in November 1963, and cut up by Arnott Young, Old Kilpatrick in June 1964.

Ex-Great Central Railway 'D11' class BR No 62667 also carried this name.

LNER 'J36' class BR No 65222 SOMME is seen at Polmont depot on 19 August 1958. *Norman Preedy Archive*

Somme. At the start of 1916, most of the British Army was an inexperienced and patchily trained body of volunteers. The Somme was the major test for Kitchener's Army. The British volunteers were often the fittest, most enthusiastic, and best educated citizens, but were also inexperienced soldiers. British casualties on the first day were the worst in the history of the British Army, with 57,470 British casualties, 19,240 of whom were killed.

The Thiepval Memorial to the Missing of the Somme. For the dead of the Somme battles of World War I who have no known grave. It was designed by Sir Edwin Lutyens and unveiled by Edward Prince of Wales on 1 August 1932. An inscription reads 'Here are recorded names of officers and men of the British Armies who fell on the Somme battlefields July 1915 to February 1918 but to whom the fortune of war denied the known and honoured burial given to their comrades in death.' *Rolf Kranz*

65224 (NBR 648, LNER 9648 – 5224 – 1946 number) built at Cowlairs Works. Entered traffic in February 1891. Named MONS after returning from ROD service, 1919. Withdrawn by BR in May 1963, and cut up by T.W. Ward, Inverkeithing in March 1964.

Ex-Great Central Railway 'D11' class BR No 62665 also carried this name.

LNER 'J36' class BR No 65224 MONS is seen at Haymarket shed in 1958. *Norman Preedy Archive*

Mons. Britain declared war on Germany on 4 August 1914 and on 9 August, the BEF began embarking for France. The Battle of Mons was the first major action of the British Expeditionary Force (BEF) in the First World War, 23 August 1914.

Nicknamed the 'Eighteen Inchers' in reference to the diameter of the cylinders, the 'J36' engines proved to be a very useful and reliable class, and although primarily freight locomotives they were often rostered to work branch, and on rare occasions main line passenger trains. From the initial total of 123 locomotives taken into BR stock, despite steady scrapping, 75 were reported as serviceable at the end of 1960. Six were still busy at work in May 1966 and the last two were finally withdrawn in 1967. Those two engines had the distinction of outlasting all other Scottish steam, including later LNER and BR designs.

65226 (NBR 650, LNER 9650–5226 – 1946 number) built at Cowlairs Works. Entered traffic in April 1891. Named HAIG after returning from ROD service, 1919. Withdrawn by BR in April 1951, and cut up at Inverurie Locomotive Works, in May 1951.

This name was also carried by 'J36'class BR No 65311.

LNER 'J36' class BR No 65226 HAIG is seen as LNER 5226 and then unnamed at Kipps depot circa 1947. *Rail Photoprints Collection*

Haig. Field Marshal Douglas Haig, 1st Earl Haig, KT, GCB, OM, GCVO, KCIE (19 June 1861–29 January 1928) was a senior officer of the British Army.

Haig seen as a Hussar age 23, February 1885.

Field Marshal Douglas Haig, 1st Earl Haig.

65233 (NBR 657, LNER 9657–5233 – 1946 number) built at Cowlairs Works. Entered traffic in July 1891. Named PLUMER after returning from ROD service, 1919. Withdrawn by BR in December 1960, and cut up at Inverurie Locomotive Works, in December 1960.

LNER 'J36' class BR No 65233 PLUMER is seen at Bathgate depot circa 1955. *Norman Preedy Archive*

Plumer. Field Marshal Herbert Charles Onslow Plumer, 1st Viscount Plumer, GCB, GCMG, GCVO, GBE (13 March 1857–16 July 1932) was a senior British Army officer.

Plumer was a Field Marshal and an officer in the York and Lancaster Regiment. Appointed to command the 2nd Corps from May 1915, he succeeded in holding Ypres on the Western Front and captured Messines by trench and mine warfare. He was arguably the most liked and trusted of the World War I military leaders. He was appointed Governor of Malta in May 1919. In July of that year he was promoted to Field Marshal. In October 1925 he was appointed High Commissioner of the British Mandate for Palestine and created Viscount Plumer of Messines on 3 June 1929. Plumer died at his home in Knightsbridge, London on 16 July 1952 and his body was subsequently interred at Westminster Abbey.

Alessio Ascalesi the Archbishop of Naples, 1st Viscount Plumer, Luigi Barlassina the Latin Patriarch of Jerusalem are seen together in Jerusalem on 11 August 1926. *American Colony (Jerusalem) photographer*

65235 (NBR 659, LNER 9659–5235 – 1946 number) built at Cowlairs Works. Entered traffic in August 1891. Named GOUGH after returning from ROD service, 1919. Withdrawn by BR in October 1961, and cut up by Arnott Young, Old Kilpatrick in June 1963.

LNER 'J36' class BR No 65235 GOUGH is seen adjacent to Murrayfield Stadium on 16 October 1955. Note that the locomotive's home shed Haymarket is stencilled on the buffer beam. *David Anderson*

Gough. General Sir Hubert de la Poer Gough GCB, GCMG, KCVO (12 August 1870–18 March 1963) was a senior officer in the British Army.

Appointed to lead the 5th Army during the Somme offence in 1916, and at Passchendaele in the following year, his reportedly less than effective command and the manner of it, contributed to high casualty figures bringing about the collapse of the 5th Army. Gough officially retired from the British Army as a full General on 26 October 1922. From 1936 until 1943, Gough was honorary colonel of the 16th/5th The Queen's Royal Lancers, at the insistence of the regiments concerned. In May 1940 Gough joined the Local Defence Volunteers (LDV–Home Guard) and was put in command of the Chelsea area unit, which he organised from scratch. News of his efficient performance reached Churchill's ears, and in June 1940 he was soon promoted to Zone Commander Fulham & Chelsea. Gough helped to found, and was president of, the Irish Servicemen's Shamrock Club, which opened in March 1943 off Park Lane, London W.1, with a grant of £1,000 from the Guinness Brewing Company. Gough died in London on 18 March 1963 and was cremated at Golders Green Crematorium.

Gough (far left) is seen conversing with King Albert I of Belgium during a visit to the Western Front.

84

LNER 'J36' class BR No 65235 GOUGH is seen whilst shunting coal wagons at Seafield depot Edinburgh during June 1950. *J. Davenport/Norman Preedy Archive*

LNER 'J36' class BR No 65235 GOUGH is seen at Haymarket depot in the company of 'D11' class locomotives BR No 62679 LORD GLENALLAN to the right, and BR No 62692 ALLAN-BANE to the rear, in this 1954 image. *David Anderson*

65236 (NBR 660, LNER 9660–5236 – 1946 number) built at Cowlairs Works. Entered traffic in August 1891. Named HORNE after returning from ROD service, 1919. Withdrawn by BR in April 1956, and cut up at Inverurie Locomotive Works in May 1956.

The centre wheel splasher of BR No 65236 HORNE with the stencilled locomotive name and Cowlairs Works makers plate. *Norman Preedy Archive*

Horne. General Henry Sinclair Horne, 1st Baron Horne, GCB, KCMG (19 February 1861–14 August 1929) was a military officer in the British Army. He was the only British artillery officer to command an army in World War I. Horne commanded the British First Army from September 1916 until the World War I Armistice, 1918. He was promoted to Lieutenant Colonel in 1905 after being commissioned into the Royal Artillery in which regiment he served during the South African War. Attached to Haig's 1st Corps in France at the outbreak of war in August 1914 as commander of an artillery brigade, he was later posted to Egypt. On his return to France in 1916, Horne's 15th Corps played a significant role in the Battle of the Somme in July 1916 with other successes at Vimy Ridge and at Arras.

He was knighted in 1916 and created Baron of Stirkoke in the County of Caithness. On 30 July 1920, Horne was appointed a deputy lieutenant of Caithness. He was appointed Master Gunner of St. James's Park, an honorary position he would hold until his death; he was also appointed Colonel of the Highland Light Infantry. He retired from the British Army in 1923. Horne died suddenly and unexpectedly at his home on 14 August 1929.

General Horne is seen inspecting the 24th Motor Machine Gun Battalion at Dieval, 12 June 1918. The motorbikes are Clyno 744 cc twin cylinder machines fitted with a sidecar and Vickers machine-guns. *David McLellan, (2nd Lieutenant)*

LNER 'J36' class BR No 65236 HORNE is seen with sister engines, as LNER No 9660 at Kipps depot in 1936. *Mike Morant Collection*

LNER 'J36' class BR No 65236 HORNE is seen again at Kipps on 26 July 1953. *RCTS Archive*

65243 (NBR 673, LNER 9673 – 5243 – 1946 number) built by Neilson & Company, Works No 4392. Entered traffic in December 1891. Named MAUDE after returning from ROD service, 1919. Withdrawn by BR in July 1966, and saved for preservation. **P**

Preserved LNER 'J36' class BR No 65243 MAUDE is seen as North British Railway No 673 whilst standing at Inverkeithing with a special to Edinburgh Waverley, on 4 May 1980. *David Anderson*

Ex-North British Railway (NBR) 'C' class locomotive BR No 65243 MAUDE (LNER 'J36' class) worked on freight duties until being withdrawn from service at Bathgate depot in July 1966, after a revenue earning service life of 74 years and 7 months. Following an appeal by the Scottish Railway Preservation Society (SRPS) the locomotive was saved from the cutter's torch and restored to working order over a 3-year period. It was repainted in the goods livery of the NBR and enjoyed a new lease of life hauling special trains and also visiting heritage railway lines. After the expiry of its boiler certificate, the 2F 2-cylinder 0-6-0 locomotive was again retired from service and placed on static display. In 2019 the cosmetically restored engine was recorded as being on display at the SRPS Museum at Bo'ness. In the future it is planned to again restore the 'J36' to working order.

LNER 'J36' class BR No 65243 MAUDE is seen at Haymarket depot on 6 May 1956. *David Anderson*

Maude. Lieutenant General Sir Frederick Stanley Maude KCB, CMG, DSO (24 June 1864–18 November 1917) was a British Army officer. His father was Sir Frederick Francis Maude, a general who had been awarded the Victoria Cross in 1855 during the Crimean War.

Maude commanded troops on the Mesopotamia front during World War I. Born in Gibraltar, he entered Sandhurst after education at Eton College and joined the Coldstream Guards. He reached the rank of Colonel and was further promoted to Brigadier General with command of the 14th Brigade in France. After recuperation of wounds received in April 1915, Maude became Major General in June of that year and took command of the 33rd Division in England. Further commands saw actions at Suvia, Gallipoli and in Mesopotamia, culminating in conflicts against the Turks in the capture of Baghdad in 1917. Maude died of cholera 18 November 1917 and is buried in Baghdad North Gate War Cemetery. His name is also noted on a memorial in Brompton Cemetery, London. An equestrian statue of Maude was unveiled in December 1923 in Baghdad however, that effigy was torn down in 1958 following the removal of the Iraqi monarchy.

Maude's equestrian statue in Baghdad circa 1939.

Sir Frederick Stanley Maude. *Illustrated London News*

LNER 'J36' class BR No 65243 MAUDE is seen at Bathgate depot on 31 August 1964. The locomotive was withdrawn from this depot. *Mike Morant Collection*

Preserved LNER 'J36' class BR No 65243 MAUDE is seen as North British Railway No 673 whilst departing from Inverkeithing on 4 May 1980 with the SRPS Clyde Coast Express. *David Anderson*

The routes were: Falkirk Grahamston–Larbert
Larbert–Falkirk Grahamston–Edinburgh Waverley
Edinburgh Waverley–Inverkeithing and return
Edinburgh Waverley–Falkirk Grahamston–Larbert
Larbert–Falkirk Grahamston

Preserved LNER 'J36' class BR No 65243 MAUDE is seen as North British Railway No 673 passing through the Blackburn area during its journey from Falkirk to Rainhill, for the Rainhill Celebrations 17 May 1980. *Colin Whitfield/Rail Photoprints*

Preserved LNER 'J36' class BR No 65243 MAUDE is seen as North British Railway No 673 whilst running through the sidings alongside Blackburn station following its servicing stop on its way to the Rainhill Celebrations. The Rainhill event took place on 24/25 and 26 May 1980. *Colin Whitfield/Rail Photoprints*

65253 (NBR 682, LNER 9682–5253 – 1946 number) built by Sharp Stewart, Works No 3772. Entered traffic in February 1892. Named JOFFRE after returning from ROD service, 1919. Withdrawn by BR in May 1963, and cut up at Inverurie Locomotive Works in August 1963.

LNER 'J36' class BR No 65253 JOFFRE is seen at its then home shed of Dunfermline circa 1949. *J. Davenport/Norman Preedy Archive*

Joffre. Marshal Joseph Jacques Césaire Joffre (12 January 1852–3 January 1931) was a French Army General.

Joffre served as Commander-in-Chief of French forces on the Western Front from the start of World War I until the end of 1916. He is best known for regrouping the retreating allied armies to defeat the Germans at the First Battle of the Marne in September 1914. His political position waned after unsuccessful offensives in 1915, the German attack on Verdun in 1916, and the disappointing results of the Anglo-French offensive on the Somme in 1916. At the end of 1916 he was promoted to Marshal of France, and moved to an advisory role, from which he quickly resigned.

Joffre's popularity with his troops led to his nickname Papa Joffre. He died on 3 January 1931 in Paris and was buried on his estate in Louveciennes.

Marshal Joseph Jacques Césaire Joffre.

Statue of Joffre in Chantilly erected in 1930.

65268 (NBR 611, LNER 9611–5268 – 1946 number) built at Cowlairs Works. Entered traffic in August 1892. Named ALLENBY after returning from ROD service, 1919. Withdrawn by BR in November 1962, and cut up at Inverurie Locomotive Works in January 1963.

LNER 'J36' class BR No 65268 ALLENBY is seen at Eastfield depot in 1949. *Rail Photoprints Collection*

Allenby. Field Marshal Edmund Henry Hynman Allenby, 1st Viscount Allenby, GCB, GCMG, GCVO (23 April 1861–14 May 1936) was a British Army officer and British Imperial Governor.

Allenby was commissioned in 1882 and served in the Boer War. He rose to command a cavalry column and was appointed Inspector General of Cavalry in 1909. In 1914 during World War I, he led a cavalry division in France with distinction. As the commander of the 3rd Army from 1915, he directed forces at the Battle of Arras before being transferred to oppose the Turkish forces in Palestine where he captured Damascus. In 1919 he was appointed Special High Commissioner of Egypt and on 31 July of that year he was made Field Marshal. He was created Viscount Allenby of Megiddo (northern Israel) and Felixstowe in the county of Suffolk on 7 October 1919. He died suddenly in London on 14 May 1936 and was cremated with his ashes being buried in Westminster Abbey.

Field Marshal Edmund Henry Hynman Allenby, 1st Viscount Allenby is seen in an image created on 11 December 1917.

LNER 'J36' class BR No 65268 ALLENBY is seen at Bathgate depot on 3 August 1952. Note that the locomotive tender was not repainted as BR at that time.
B.K.B. Green/Norman Preedy Archive

LNER 'J36' class BR No 65268 ALLENBY with steam to spare passes with a freight working at Gorgie on the Edinburgh Suburban Line on 9 May 1953.
David Anderson

LNER 'J36' class BR No 65268 ALLENBY is seen at Haymarket depot, late 1953 and with a BR early logo on the tender. *David Anderson*

65311 (NBR 753, LNER 9753–5311 – 1946 number) built at Cowlairs Works. Entered traffic in March 1899. Named HAIG previously carried by BR No 65226 and reallocated in June 1955. Withdrawn by BR in November 1963, and cut up by Arnott Young, Old Kilpatrick during June 1964.

This name was previously carried by 'J36' BR No 65226 which was scrapped in 1951.

LNER 'J36' class BR No 65311 HAIG is seen at Craigentinny depot on 24 July 1955. *Norman Preedy Archive*

Chapter 3

60163 TORNADO – 50TH MEMBER OF THE LEGENDARY 'A1' PACIFIC CLASS

60163 TORNADO built by A1 Trust at Hopetown Works, Darlington as No 2195. First steamed 11 January 2008. Publicly launched 1 August 2008. First passenger train hauled 21 September 2008 at the Great Central Railway. Final mainline test run 19 November 2008. First passenger journey on the UK mainline 31 January 2009. Officialy named 19 February 2009 at York.

A1 Pacific (4-6-2) No 60163 is seen after being named TORNADO. On that occasion HRH Prince Charles, Prince of Wales was in the driving seat during a mainline run. The new A1 is seen passing Colton with the Royal Train. The British Railways class A1 number series ran from 60113 to 60162, and the new locomotive was given what would have been the next number in that series. *Fred Kerr*

In 1990 a group of people came together to share what was at that time considered to be an extraordinary ambition, to construct a brand-new 3-cylinder Peppercorn A1 Pacific. They formed the A1 Steam Locomotive Trust and after nineteen years of incredible effort and considerable expenditure, the new locomotive No 60163 TORNADO moved under its own power for the first time in August 2008. The new-build Pacific celebrated its 10th anniversary in August 2018. At the start of 2009 perhaps the most impressive preservation milestone ever, was passed when the newly built A1 Class 4-6-2 made the first of what turned out to be many mainline runs.

The superbly engineered machine was the first standard gauge steam locomotive built in the UK since British Railways Standard 9F 2-10-0 No. 92220 EVENING STAR rolled out of Swindon Locomotive Works on 18 March 1960. Accordingly, it was also the first express passenger locomotive to be built in Britain since the unique British Railways Pacific No 71000 DUKE OF GLOUCESTER left Crewe Locomotive Works in 1954.

The project to build a 50th member of the long-lamented Peppercorn A1 Pacific class locomotive, using 21st century steam technology, reportedly cost in the region of £3 million. The A1 heralded a 'new build' mainline steam locomotive era in the UK, a movement which then continued to gain momentum.

The Tornado nameplate carries the crest of RAF station Cottesmore. *Fred Kerr*

The Peppercorn A1 class

The LNER A1 class Pacific locomotives were designed by Arthur H. Peppercorn, the last Chief Mechanical Engineer (CME) of the London & North Eastern Railway. They were the last in a line of famous express passenger steam locomotives built for use on the East Coast Main Line (ECML) an auspicious list which included the Stirling Singles, the Ivatt Atlantics, and the Gresley A4 Pacific class.

The original 49 Peppercorn Class A1s were ordered by the LNER and built at Doncaster Works (26 locos) and Darlington Works (23 locos) for British Railways (BR) between 1948 and 1949, the first two years of railway nationalisation.

Equipped with a huge 50sq foot fire grate, the locos were able to use lower grade coal than their predecessors. They first ran without names, but eventually they all carried names on the side of their smoke deflectors. The Peppercorn engines were originally fitted with plain topped (un-lipped) double chimney castings which were eventually changed for lipped chimneys, a change that in the opinions of many greatly improved the look of the class.

The A1 class engines were heralded as being excellent performers by engine crews; and as intended they ran and steamed well even on relatively poor-quality coal. They also fulfilled the designer's intentions with regard to low maintenance requirements, in fact reportedly needing less routine maintenance than any of the other express locomotives running on BR at the time of their introduction.

Five of the 'A1s' (Nos 60153–60157) were fitted with Timken roller bearings on all of their axles. These had already been tried successfully on some of the 'A4' loco tenders. The bearings were trialed with the intention of further increasing the period between heavy repairs. Although the roller bearing experiment was judged a success the fitting of them was never expanded to include other members of the class.

An undesirable side effect with the A1 class Kylchap exhaust arrangement was the loud operating sound of the associated ejectors when used whilst standing in the station, as the noise was reportedly loud enough to drown out tannoy announcements to passengers. As a result, silencers were fitted experimentally, and were found to be effective. Livery styles used included LNER apple green, BR Brunswick green, the pre-1957 shade and also BR Brunswick green post 1957 shade, and also BR blue.

Withdrawal of the class started with BR No 60123 H.A. IVATT in October 1962 after an accident, and by the end of 1964 only 26 of the class remained in service. The last two Peppercorn 'A1' class engines were withdrawn in 1966. No example was saved for preservation.

Peppercorn A1 class Pacific BR No 60162 HOLYROOD is pictured standing under the bridge which carried the former Caledonian Railway Leith North and Granton lines over the Edinburgh Waverley to Glasgow Queen Street mainline. The locomotive is preparing to back down to Waverley station to work an Aberdeen express during September 1957. *David Anderson*

The A1 Trust Locomotive

From the very beginning the Trust regarded TORNADO not as a replica or copy of any one of its 49 predecessors, but as the fiftieth A1. This simple decision gave the Trust licence to make small changes to the design to better suit modern manufacturing techniques and to fit in with modern high-speed railway operating procedures, while remaining demonstrably faithful to the greater part of the original design.

The principal change from the original design concerned the boiler. The locomotive boiler was designed as a fully welded vessel with a steel firebox, as opposed to the original A1 design, which was of a riveted construction married to a traditional copper firebox.

Requirements for modern operating conditions were a major part of the new locomotive design.

The original A1 class locomotives were equipped with a steam brake for the locomotive and vacuum brake for the train. As it was intended that the new locomotive would spend most of its operating time on the national network (main line) the Trust decided to specify air brakes as its primary braking system for the locomotive. To enable No 60163 to haul vacuum braked stock on heritage railways, a vacuum ejector was fitted with the vacuum train pipe being controlled through an air/vacuum proportional valve. In addition to the automatic fail-safe air brake system, the locomotive is also equipped with a straight air brake to assist with shunting and coupling operations.

The original locomotives were fitted with the BR vacuum brake AWS (Automatic Warning System).

To suit modern mainline service TORNADO required the new generation of TPWS (Train Protection and Warning System) to be fitted. Modern operating conditions also require that a data recorder be fitted on all motive power running on Network Rail. Cab to lineside radio equipment was also fitted. Therefore, a modern electric power generating system with associated batteries was installed.

The A1 class locomotive tender has been redesigned internally eliminating the water scoop (as fitted to the original A1 locomotives) but increasing the water capacity from 5000 gallons (22,700 litres) to around 6,200 gallons (28,150 litres) and correspondingly reducing coal capacity from 9 tons to 7.5 tons. The range of a steam locomotive is governed by water capacity, lubricant consumption and fuel capacity.

Water is the most significant limitation with most locomotives hauling loaded trains at express speeds being limited to about 100 miles (160 km) between fillings of the tender. The original A1 class averaged 40–45 gallons (113–137 litres) of water used per mile. Thus, the standard 5000 gallons (22,700 litres) capacity of the tender allowed an average travel of approximately 100 miles (160 km), and allowed for 500 gallons (2,270 litres) in reserve. With the capacity of the TORNADO tender augmented to 6,200 gallons (27,240 litres) plus a proposed 8,000 gallons (36,320 litres) in a possible second coupled vehicle, a range of around 300 miles (480 km) non-stop could be achievable. That capacity would allow operation from Euston to Carlisle (WCML) or Kings Cross to Newcastle (ECML).

In comparison the steam era 'Elizabethan' non-stop runs between London Kings Cross and Edinburgh Waverley totalled approximately 400 miles (640 km), including the shed movements at either end of the journey. The A1 class was designed to cope with the heaviest regular East Coast trains of the post-war period. Those were regularly loaded to 15 coaches with which the locomotives were capable of maintaining 60–70 miles per hour (95–110 km/hr) on level track. However, the greatest asset of TORNADO will be the ability to haul lighter (10–11 coach trains) at higher speeds, to comply with modern traffic patterns.

TORNADO is pictured in grey primer whilst undergoing running trials at the Great Central Railway (GCR) on 4 October 2008. The special tender design can clearly be seen in this image. *Andrew Smith*

TORNADO is seen posed at the Great Central Railway in October 2008. Note the lipped double chimney and also the lighting generator located behind the right-hand smoke deflector. *Clive Hanley*

TORNADO is about to back down on to a train at the Great Central Railway, Loughborough in October 2008. The new locomotive carries the LNER route availability indication 'RA9' on the cabside door, denoting a locomotive with an axle load of 24.1 tonne. *Clive Hanley*

The TORNADO footplate. Above, the driver's side of the cab on which the speedometer, vacuum gauges, red painted regulator and train brake controls can all clearly be seen. *Clive Hanley*

A general view of the footplate showing the boiler management controls, reverser and closed firebox door. *Clive Hanley*

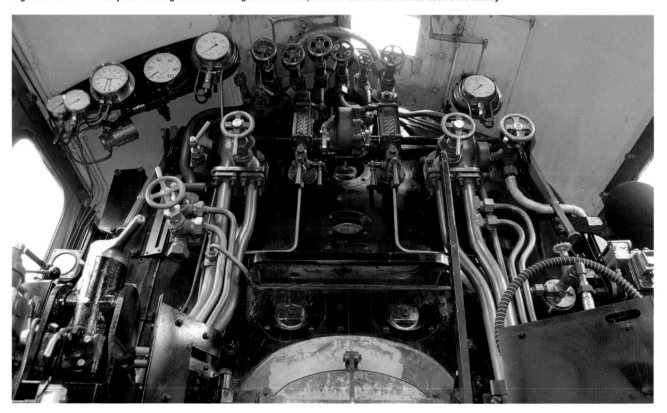

A1 Trust Pacific No 60163 TORNADO is seen outside the main display hall at the National Railway Museum (NRM) York. The locomotive is in light steam having been prepared for a forthcoming outing on the mainline during October 2010. Modern high-intensity train lamps are fitted and they are located on top of the locomotive's outer two buffer beam electric lamps, note also the top mounted locomotive lamp (4 front train lamps in total). *Fred Kerr*

TORNADO

A Panavia Tornado variable sweep wing, multirole combat aircraft is seen whilst landing at RAF Fairford, Gloucester during August 2007. *Pete Skelton*

The A1 Trust Peppercorn 4-6-2 Pacific was not the first mainline locomotive to carry the name. British Railways Standard Britannia Pacific No 70022 built at Crewe Works in 1951 also carried the name. The origin of the designation in that instance was more in keeping the commonly accepted dictionary description. Tornado, n. local tropical thunderstorm; hurricane; whirling tempest.

A Royal Navy 'R-class' destroyer named HMS *Tornado* was operational in World War I. She was sunk, with the loss of 80 of her complement of 82 crew in 1917, after striking a German mine.

However, the A1 Trust locomotive was named for the RAF crews flying the Panavia Tornado aircraft at that time and specifically during the Gulf War (1990–1991).

The Panavia Tornado is a family of twin-engine, variable-sweep wing multirole combat aircraft, which was jointly developed and manufactured by Italy, the United Kingdom, and West Germany. There are three primary Tornado variants which are Tornado IDS (interdictor/strike) fighter-bomber, the suppression of enemy air defences, the Tornado ECR (electronic combat/reconnaissance) and the Tornado ADV (air defence variant) interceptor aircraft.

The Tornado was developed and built by Panavia Aircraft GmbH, a tri-national consortium consisting of British Aerospace (previously British Aircraft Corporation), MBB of West Germany, and Aeritalia of Italy. It first flew on 14 August 1974 and was introduced into service in 1979–1980. Due to its multirole design, it was able to replace several different fleets of aircraft in the adopting air forces.

The Royal Saudi Air Force (RSAF) became the only export operator of the Tornado in addition to the three original partner nations. A tri-nation training and evaluation unit operating from RAF Cottesmore, the Tri-National Tornado Training Establishment, maintained a level of international co-operation beyond the production stage.

The Tornado was operated by the Royal Air Force (RAF), Italian Air Force, and RSAF during the Gulf War of 1991, in which the Tornado conducted many low-altitude penetrating strike missions. The Tornados of various services were also used in conflicts in the former Yugoslavia during the Bosnian War and Kosovo War, the Iraq War, Libya during the Libyan civil war, as well as smaller roles in Afghanistan, Yemen, and Syria. Including all variants, a total 992 aircraft were built.

Following the withdrawal of the RAF's Tornado F3 fleet from service in 2010, BAE Systems created the 'Reduce to Produce' programme. The scheme, based at RAF Leeming in Yorkshire, stripped down the decommissioned F3 fleet and recycled parts that can be used as spares for the UK's in-service GR4 fleet. The scheme was designed to help cut costs on support for the Tornado Squadrons whilst still maintaining a fully comprehensive spares supply chain for the aircrafts. It was reportedly a resounding success since its introduction, with the engineers able to recover between 800–1200 parts per airframe creating a huge saving for the RAF.

GR4 Tornado – Capability Statistics,
Engines: Two Rolls Royce RB199 MK103 turbofans.
Thrust: 16,000lbs each.
Max Altitude: 50,000ft
Max Speed: 1.3 Mach

RB199 engine on display at RAF Cosford. *Len Mills*

The RAF have for sometime used a designated low fly zone in Mid Wales referred to as the Machynlleth Loop (Mach Loop for short) for low level flight training. It is so named due its proximity to the Powys town of the same name, and is also near to the town of Dolgellau.

Tornado G4 'ZA597/063' from RAF Marham, Norfolk streaks through the Machynlleth Loop during the Tornado's last autumn with the RAF on 25 September 2018. *Michael Brazier*

Tornado G4 'ZD719/085' then from RAF Marham, is seen flying the Mach Loop on 22 May 2012. This aircraft was scrapped in July 2014. *John Styles*

RAF Marham GR4 Tornado aircraft 'ZA614/076' seen in and around the base on 13 November 2018. *John Styles*

A Tornado from II (AC) Squadron, RAF Marham, flies over the Shard skyscraper building in London during Her Majesty the Queen's 2013 birthday fly-past. This image was a winner in the RAF's Photographic Competition 2013. Tornado 'ZE116/116' was scrapped 7 November 2013. *SAC Andy Masson/MOD*

RAF Tornado GR4 aircraft 'ZD744/092' pictured over Iraq on an armed reconnaissance mission in support of OP SHADER on 27 September 2014. *Cpl Neil Bryden RAF/MOD*

2008

New Peppercorn A1 Trust Pacific No 60163 TORNADO is seen in action at the Great Central Railway (GCR) during an October gala event in 2008. *Clive Hanley*

The new 3-cylinder A1 Trust Pacific with a lipped double chimney makes a fine sight as it stands in the display area main hall of the National Railway Museum having been given an LNER Apple Green livery on 1 January 2009, and prior to being named. The chime whistle and lighting generator can both be seen located inside the right-hand smoke deflector. Note the 51A Darlington shedplate. *Phil Brown*

New A1 No 60163 TORNADO approaches Kimbridge Crossing with 1Z94 the 09.40 Waterloo–Waterloo via Andover, Laverstolck, Southamton and Eastleigh 'The Cathedrals Express' working, on 14 February 2009. *John Chalcraft/Rail Photoprints*

The St. Mary Bourne viaduct at Hurstbourne forms part of the main railway line between Salisbury and London and was constructed in the mid-19th century. It carries the railway over the valley of Bourne Rivulet which is a tributary of the River Test. New A1 No 60163 TORNADO crosses Hurstbourne Viaduct with 1Z94 the 09.40 Waterloo via Andover, Laverstock, Southampton and Eastleigh, on 14 February 2009. *John Chalcraft/Rail Photoprints*

The location is the yard at Barrow Hill Roundhouse on 3 April 2009. *David Gibson*

An impressive LNER line up left to right, 'A1' TORNADO, 'A2' BR No 60532 BLUE PETER, 'A4' BR No 60007 SIR NIGEL GRESLEY, 'A4' BR No 60009 UNION OF SOUTH AFRICA and 'K1' BR No 62005. Note that the locomotive was at that time fitted with an un-lipped double chimney. *David Gibson*

Barrow Hill engine shed is a former Midland Railway steam round house which until 1948 was called Staveley Roundhouse. The shed is at Barrow Hill near Chesterfield, Derbyshire. It was saved by the members of the Barrow Hill Engine Shed Society when the shed was closed by British Rail in 1991.

The Barrow Hill engine shed re-opened under society ownership in July 1998. This is the only roundhouse left where preserved and now 'new build' steam locomotives can be seen and demonstrated close to the viewing enthusiasts. After an impressive refurbishment and the creation of a railway visitor centre a gala event was held on 23 September 2017 to mark the re-opening of the Barrow Hill Roundhouse.

Both 'A1' No 60163 TORNADO and 'A3' BR No 60163 FLYING SCOTSMAN were there on that occasion.

Night time at Barrow Hill on 3 April 2009. Tornado is in the company of 'A2' BR No 60532 BLUE PETER. *Fred Kerr*

Tornado is additionally in the company of 'A4' class locomotives BR No 60009 UNION OF SOUTH AFRICA and BR No 60007 SIR NIGEL GRESLEY. *Fred Kerr*

The North Yorkshire Moors Railway is a heritage railway in North Yorkshire. The heritage line is located along the route of the former Whitby and Pickering Railway. That railway was planned by George Stephenson in 1831, opened in 1836 and closed by BR in 1965. The heritage railway was opened in 1973 by the North York Moors Historical Railway Trust Ltd. The preserved line is a significant tourist attraction which has been awarded many industry accolades.

No 60163 is seen leaving Goathland on 6 May 2009. *David Gibson*

TORNADO is seen in a typical NYMR picturesque setting, on this occasion at Darnholme on 6 May 2009. *David Gibson*

Goathland railway station is almost unchanged since its construction in 1865. The station has been restored to represent a North Eastern Railway (NER) country station circa 1922. The location is popular with tourists due to its appearances in Yorkshire TV's Heartbeat series and also in the first of the Harry Potter films.

TORNADO is seen passing the impressive period signal array leaving Goathland with a photographic charter train for Pickering on Wednesday 6 May 2009. As can be seen on that occasion the signals were not in use. *David Gibson*

A1 Trust Pacific No 60163 TORNADO makes a volcanic start as it passes Bedminster, Bristol with 1Z29, the 15.34 Gloucester–Minehead 'Severn Coast Express' operated by Pathfinder Tours on 30 May 2009. *John Chalcraft/Rail Photoprints*

A1 Pacific No 60163 TORNADO approaches Bristol with the 1Z28 the 12.41 Cardiff–Bristol 'Severn Coast Express' operated by Pathfinder Tours, on 30 May 2009. *John Chalcraft/Rail Photoprints*

New Build A1 Trust Pacific No 60163 TORNADO is seen alongside the River Severn at Gatcombe, Gloucestershire with charter train 1Z29 'Severn Coast Express' operated by Pathfinder Tours, on 30 May 2009. *Pete Skelton*

A1 Trust Pacific No 60163 TORNADO leaves Bristol Temple Meads at the head of the first 'Torbay Express' (09.15 Bristol–Kingswear) of the summer season, 5 July 2009. By this period in time the locomotive had clocked up 10,000 miles in service. *John Chalcraft /Rail Photoprints*

Locomotive No 60163 TORNADO seen in early evening light at Bristol TM after arrival from Kingswear with a return 'Torbay Express', on 12 July 2009. *John Chalcraft Rail Photoprints*

A1 Trust No 60163 TORNADO seen at Settle on the S&C route with a York–Carlisle charter carrying 'The Waverley' headboard, on 4 October 2009. *Fred Kerr*

A1 No 60163 TORNADO seen at Appleby on the S&C route with a Worcester – Carlisle working, on 10 October 2009. *Fred Kerr*

TORNADO waits at Preston prior to departing for Crewe with its support coach at 20.19 on 10 October 2009. *Fred Kerr*

A1 No 60163 TORNADO at the Severn Valley Railway (SVR). The locomotive is seen at a gala event on 28 October 2009 whilst hauling that railway's superbly restored set of LNER Gresley teak coaches.

Passing Chelmarsh. *Fred Kerr*

At Northwood. *Fred Kerr*

2010

A1 Trust No 60163 TORNADO arrives at the Museum of Science and Industry (MOSI) Manchester on 4 February 2010 after conveying HRH Prince of Wales and the Duchess of Cornwall from Preston during Royal visits to the North West of England. Note the royal headlamp code consists of three lamps on the buffer beam complemented by the Prince of Wales feathers and flags. The normal four lamp royal head code is only carried when the Monarch travels on the Royal Train. *Fred Kerr*

Locomotive No 60163 TORNADO is seen with the Royal Train at Manchester Victoria station on 4 February 2010. The unlipped chimney style can clearly be seen in this image. *Fred Kerr*

A1 Trust No 60163 TORNADO is again seen with the Royal Train at Manchester Victoria station on 4 February 2010. Diesel locomotive No 67005 QUEENS MESSENGER is attached to the rear. *Fred Kerr*

A1 Trust Pacific 60163 TORNADO is seen passing Acton Turville with 1Z88 the 08.45 London Victoria–Swansea 'Cathedrals Express', on 1 March 2010. *John Chalcraft/Rail Photoprints*

A1 Trust Pacific No 60163 TORNADO is seen passing Rimington with a Carlisle–Crewe charter (Trust headboard carried) on 14 April 2010. *Fred Kerr*

A1 Pacific 60163 TORNADO is seen at Greenholme (WCML) on 24 June 2010 with the Crewe–Carlisle leg of the 'Border Raider' charter. During this run TORNADO beat the previous record for the fastest steam hauled railtour over Shap Summit by 19 seconds. Both images *Fred Kerr*

No 60163 is seen after crossing the famous Ribblehead viaduct with the Carlisle–Crewe leg of the 'Border Raider' on 24 June 2010. The Ribblehead Viaduct or Batty Moss Viaduct carries the Settle–Carlisle Railway across Batty Moss in the Ribble Valley at Ribblehead, in North Yorkshire. The viaduct, built by the Midland Railway is a Grade II listed structure. *Fred Kerr*

TORNADO is seen again with the Carlisle–Crewe leg of the 'Border Raider' on 24 June 2010. On this occasion the location is Langho. *Fred Kerr*

A1 Trust Pacific No 60163 TORNADO is seen being coaled and prepared for action, during the North Yorkshire Moors Railway Autumn Gala on 1 October 2010. *Phil Brown*

A1 Trust Pacific No 60163 TORNADO carries 'The East Lancs Tornado' headboard during a 27 October 2010 visit to that railway and is seen at Burrs. *Fred Kerr*

2011

In January 2011 the locomotive's boiler was sent to DB Meiningen, Germany for repairs. When TORNADO returned to service it carried a newly applied BR Brunswick Green lined livery and as can be seen a lipped style double chimney. The tender carried the early BR 'Lion on a Bike' logo. No 60163 TORNADO is seen at the North Yorkshire Moors Railway in May 2011.

Entering Grosmont Tunnel. *Phil Brown*

Leaving Grosmont. *Phil Brown*

A1 Trust Pacific No 60163 TORNADO departs Bristol Temple Meads at the head a 'Torbay Express' working (Bristol-Kingswear) on 10 July 2011. *Pete Skelton*

Back at the SVR. No 60163 TORNADO is seen at Chelmarsh Waterworks with a Severn Valley Venturer working during the railways September 2011 Gala event. *Fred Kerr*

No 60163 TORNADO is seen at Nuneaton station with 'The Cathedrals Express' on 10 September 2011. *Clive Hanley*

On 21 September 2011 A1 Trust Pacific No 60163 arrived at Glasgow Central with 1Z53 'The Caledonian Tornado' (Crewe–Glasgow). The locomotive crew are seen with officials of HF Railtours, the operator of that charter. *Fred Kerr*

A1 Trust Pacific No 60163 TORNADO prepares to leave Glasgow Central on 21 September 2011 with the return working of 'The Caledonian Tornado' 1Z55, to Crewe. *Fred Kerr*

No 60163 TORNADO is seen at Carlisle with the aforementioned train. *Fred Kerr*

Tornado is seen during a night photo-shoot at Barrow Hill on 12 April 2012. *Fred Kerr*

No 60163 TORNADO, LNER No 4464 BITTERN, LNER No 4468 MALLARD, BR No 60532 BLUE PETER and LNER No 4771 GREEN ARROW are seen at Barrow Hill on 12 April 2012. At that time the locomotive's tender has the later BR 'Ferret and Dartboard' logo. *Fred Kerr*

Now resplendent in early 'British Railways Express Passenger Blue Livery' the new build 3-cylinder Peppercorn A1 Trust Pacific TORNADO is seen between mainline charters at the Crewe Heritage Centre, on 2 June 2013. The tender carries an early BR 'Lion on a Bike' logo. *Keith Langston Collection*

On 16 June 2013 A1 Trust Pacific locomotive, No 60163 TORNADO hauled a Scottish Railway Preservation Society (SRPS) charter, Edinburgh–Stirling–Forth Circle–Edinburgh and that train is seen at Cambuskenneth, passing below the Wallace monument. The National Wallace Monument (generally known as the Wallace Monument) is a tower standing on the shoulder of the Abbey Craig, a hilltop overlooking Stirling in Scotland. It commemorates Sir William Wallace, a 13th-century Scottish hero. *Fred Kerr*

New build A1 Trust Pacific No 60163 TORNADO leaves Bath Spa with the 07.17 Waterloo–Cardiff 'Cathedrals Express' charter operated by 'Steam Dreams', on 7 September 2013. *John Chalcraft/Rail Photoprints*

A1 Trust Pacific No 60163 TORNADO is seen at speed near Kidderminster on 14 September 2013 with 1Z39 'The Cathedrals Express' London Euston–Worcester Shrub Hill. *Pete Skelton*

In September 2013 A1 Trust Pacific No 60163 TORNADO visited Barrow Hill railway centre on the occasion of the 'Doncaster 160'. *Fred Kerr*

A1 Trust Pacific No 60163 TORNADO is seen with a 'Doncaster 160' shuttle working on 29 September 2013. The locomotive is in the company of preserved 'B1' 4-6-0 BR No 61264 masquerading as class mate BR No 61002 IMPALA. *Fred Kerr*

TORNADO is seen with another 'Doncaster 160' shuttle working on the same date. *Fred Kerr*

A1 Trust Pacific No 60163 TORNADO is seen between turns at the North Yorkshire Moors Railway on 4 October 2013. *Phil Brown*

A1 Trust Pacific No 60163 TORNADO is seen at Wansford on the Nene Valley Railway (NVR) during a photographic charter run past on 1 November 2013. *Fred Kerr*

TORNADO is again seen at Wansford on the NVR during a photographic charter on 1 November 2013. *Fred Kerr*

A1 Trust Pacific No 60163 TORNADO makes a fine sight whilst crossing the River Nene at the NVR on 1 November 2013. *Fred Kerr*

A1 Trust Pacific No 60163 TORNADO in BR Express Passenger Blue livery is seen outside the shed at Didcot in April 2014. *Peter Zabek*

TORNADO is seen at Didcot in the company of 'A4' Pacific BR No 60007 SIR NIGEL GRESLEY during an April 2014 visit to the railway centre. *David A Jones*

A1 Trust Pacific No 60163 TORNADO is seen at Swanage station, about to depart with a train to Corfe Castle, in July 2014. *Barry Skeates*

A1 Trust Pacific No 60163 TORNADO is seen passing Brislington with the 'Torbay Express' outward Bristol–Kingswear working 1Z27, at 09:22 on 2 August 2015. The locomotive is again seen in LNER Apple Green livery and with post 1948 style BRITISH RAILWAYS tender markings. *Pete Skelton*

Tornado waits for the 'road' at Bewdley, Severn Valley Railway with a Kidderminster service, 9 October 2015. *Pete Skelton*

TORNADO has made several visits to the Severn Valley Railway (SVR), all of which have attracted capacity crowds with many journeys actually being sold out. The popular SVR currently runs between the towns of Bridgnorth, Shropshire and Kidderminster, Worcestershire and the approximately 16-mile route is located in the picturesque valley of the mighty River Severn. No 60163 is seen on 9 October 2015 whilst passing Northwood Lane, a popular location for both railway photographers and enthusiasts, there is a request stop halt nearby. The LNER Apple Green livery and the SVR rake of restored Gresley teak coaches are a perfect match. *Pete Skelton*

TORNADO is seen passing Sterns with a southbound train, ex Bridgnorth on 9 October 2015. *Pete Skelton*

A1 Trust Pacific No 60163 TORNADO at Bewdley SVR on 9 October 2015.

Arriving from Bridgnorth. *Pete Skelton*

Departing to Kidderminster. *Pete Skelton*

A1 Trust Pacific No 60163 TORNADO is seen again at the SVR this time on 17 October 2015.

Passing Northwood, note the splendid 'banner repeater signal' on this bi-directional line. *Clive Hanley*

Outside the Bewdley South signal box. *Clive Hanley*

A1 Trust Pacific No 60163 TORNADO is seen shortly after leaving Bristol Temple Meads with the 'Torbay Express' outward Bristol–Kingswear working 1Z27, on 4 September 2016. Note that the locomotive is on this instance carrying two headboards. *Pete Skelton*

A1 Trust Pacific No 60163 TORNADO is seen passing Upton Noble with the 'Torbay Express' outward Bristol Temple Meads–Kingswear working 1Z27 on 11 September 2016. *John Chalcraft/Rail Photoprints*

Severn Valley Railway visitor A1 Trust Pacific No 60163 TORNADO is seen in the vicinity of Orchard Farm Crossing with the 11:23 Bridgnorth–Kidderminster service on 5 November 2016. *Fred Kerr*

A1 Trust Pacific No 60163 TORNADO is seen approaching Hampton Loade station on the Severn Valley Railway with a train ex Bridgnorth in 2016. This image was taken from the 32 mm Paddock Railway a popular visitor attraction adjacent to the station. *Malcolm Whittaker*

A1 Trust Pacific No 60163 TORNADO is seen at Helwith Bridge on the S&C with the Skipton–Appleby section of a steam charter, on 16 February 2017. Coupled at the rear of the train is locomotive No 67029 ROYAL DIAMOND. *Fred Kerr*

TORNADO arrives at Chester with the London Euston–Chester 'The Christmas Cracker' 1Z81 charter on 25 November 2017. *Fred Kerr*

A1 Trust Pacific No 60163 TORNADO is seen during a 2018 visit to the SVR. The location is Hays Bridge and the train is a Kidderminster–Bridgnorth service.
Fred Kerr

Taking the curve into Northwood A1 Trust Pacific No 60163 TORNADO makes a spirited approach with a Kidderminster–Bridgnorth service on 17 March 2018.
Clive Hanley

ACKNOWLEDGEMENTS

This is a Perceptive Images 2019 © publication exclusively for Pen & Sword Books Ltd.

Additional editorial material, special images and archive documents were supplied by David Anderson, John Chalcraft, Fred Kerr, Mike Morant, Norman Preedy, John Styles and Pete Skelton.

Photographic libraries whose images have been used include the Keith Langston Collection, Mike Morant Collection, Norman Preedy Archive, Rail Photoprints Collection, Railway Correspondence and Travel Society Archive (RCTS).

Also: British Army, National Maritime Museum, Royal Air Force, US National Archive, and Wikipedia.

A book of this nature could not have been compiled without the co-operation of numerous photographers and archivists some of whom are unfortunately no longer with us but in this publication their unique images live on.

Individual photographers whose images have been used include Michael Brazier, Phil Brown, Neil Bryden, David Gibson, Clive Hanley, David A. Jones, Rolf Kranz, Andy Masson, Len Mills, Harry Mitchell, Barry Skeates, Mike Stokes Archive, Craig Tiley, Malcolm Whittaker.

Keith Langston 2019